Igniting Change

From where you are…to where you want to be

Anna Francesca Celestino

DP Publishing
Studio City, California 91604
www.ignitingchange.com

First Edition

Printed in the United States of America

Book design by Laurie Gilbert
Illustrations by Janis Wilkins

ISBN-10 1-43829-678-9
ISBN-13 978-1-43829-678-4

Library of Congress Control Number: 2008910287

This book is dedicated to my family.

You are a wellspring of love

and a house full of laughter.

Acknowledgements

I have been blessed to be loved and supported in so many ways, on this otherwise solo journey. I'm grateful for the opportunity to express my appreciation.

First, thank you to my parents for encouraging me to write by buying me the little printing press with the rubber letters and the tweezers when I started my first newspaper at ten. My mother is an inspiration and my father is an example to live by.

As for the rest of my family - Jon, Rich, Sue, Wendie, Dan, Jenna, Nick, Anthony and Jake - what an amazing gift to be loved by them, and to laugh with them as we do so often. I thank my sister, Kathy, for being there through thick and thin, and for demonstrating how to enjoy life better than anyone I know.

Don ignited my passion for exploring consciousness. I thank him for the many things I discovered while we were together, and for the companionship we still share along the way. My gratitude to Mita, Barbara, Catherine, Lauren, and Tim for their precious friendship, and to Rick for always bringing the fire.

My gratitude to Meridith who went over this manuscript with a fine tooth comb. I thank my lucky stars for Laurie, who's creativity rounded out my vision for this book. Thanks also to Janis for adding her spirit and creativity.

Deep gratitude goes to Uranda and Martin Exeter for their teachings on consciousness, and to EDL friends living those teachings around the world.

Finally, thank you to BJ, my coach, for her mastery, generosity and patience. I'll never forget how she got me over hurdles, refused to let me stop even when I cried, and was there to celebrate every milestone. Without her, this book would not exist.

Contents

Preface | *Learning to Fly* | **4**

Change | *True Change* | **12**

Fire | *Lessons from the Caveman* | **22**

Love | *Into the Now* | **36**

Proximity | *Creating a Container for Change* | **58**

Courage | *Catching the Updraft* | **90**

Tools | *Working the Process* | **122**

Vision | *Together we Rise* | **150**

Preface | Learning to Fly

*F*or as long as I can remember, I wanted to be a writer. I started a neighborhood newspaper at ten. At seventeen I was a reporter for the community newspaper, at eighteen a journalism major at the University of Michigan, and by twenty my sights were set on New York City.

Twenty is a fragile age. We make life choices based on little or no experience. I met a cute guy. He lived in California and worked in the music business. "You could come to California and write," he said. It was minus ten degrees in Michigan and a balmy seventy on the West Coast. Need I say more? It was a fork in the road and I chose that which glittered.

Soon after, the relationship took a turn for the worse and my attention was diverted from writing to survival. For the next nine years, my life played out, revealing all of my cracks and insecurities.

I got out of the relationship and into therapy. Bit by bit, I restored some semblance of order to my life. My career, which had been completely derailed, started moving in the right direction again.

It was the 80's in LA. The "new age" was burgeoning. So was my interest in spirituality. Through a bizarre set of circumstances, I met an eclectic group of people whose mission was the restoration of human consciousness. Their community was a peaceful place. (It was not a commune. Everyone had their own living quarters.) In this tranquil setting, they integrated the spiritual teachings into their daily lives. I liked what I heard, but mostly I liked the people, and so I visited their community on Sundays.

Meanwhile, I was working at The Walt Disney Company and had been assigned the task of coordinating Mickey Mouse's 60th birthday. Imagine throwing an international bash for a mouse that wasn't even real while questioning the meaning of life. I was going full tilt in two very different directions. Talk about a crossroad. It was a recipe for disaster and by the end of the year, my body gave out. I left my job and spent the next few months recuperating in Northern California's wine country. Eventually rested, I began looking for what was next.

Curious to learn more about spiritual awareness, I contacted the community I had visited earlier and asked if I could visit for a couple of months. They said yes. My two months turned into a fourteen year association, eleven of which were spent in-residence. I couldn't get enough. It was timeless knowledge about how life works. Like a university for consciousness, we studied spiritual psychology, universal laws, nutrition, healing, relationships, transformation - everything.

I met Don at the community and we were married in 1993. We shared a passion for helping others break free of limitations. We hosted an international drumming event. We developed a personal intensive called *The Life Purpose Course*. With our spiritual training, we created a six month internship program called *Building the House of Your Being*.

As time went on, I branched out and added more teachings. I learned Shadow Work®, which contains a powerful map of the mind. I learned how to read the Akashic Records or The Book of Life. I explored the multitude of ways in which the psyche can be damaged. I started giving private sessions.

I studied the work of Dr. Zecharia Sitchen, one of the few historians who can translate Sumerian texts dating from 4-5000 B.C. Don and I accompanied Dr. Sitchen to ancient sites in Syria and Lebanon and saw scrolls that seriously rattled our belief systems. Upon our return to the United States, we created an intensive called *Identity Beyond Belief.*

This wide variety of training influenced my thinking. My path began to diverge from the community in which I lived. At the same time, my private practice began to flourish. By 2000, I had reached another crossroad.

With the support of my wonderful life coach, BJ, I began to sort out my priorities. My connection to the community fell away. I quit my job, then I stopped participating in meetings, and finally I ceased attending the spiritual services. Having had such a deep devotion to the community, I processed an enormous amount of grief at every stage.

Inherent in the process was fear. If I quit my job, would I still be able to live there? If I stopped attending community meetings, would I lose my friends? If I didn't go to Sunday service, would I be burned at the stake as a heretic?

There was also no shortage of judgments or anger. How tempting to transfer the pain out there. I sensed how toxic blame would be to both the community and to myself. Instead, I made a vow to keep a current of love in my heart, no matter what. Thus was born the first step of the three-part process that became the foundation for this book. *Commit to coming from a place of love.*

Since my husband, Don, wasn't ready to leave the community, I found myself living in the midst of everything, but not participating in anything. It was very uncomfortable. However, out of this came step number two. *Find your right proximity and wait for clarity.* How close or how removed did I need to be to feel loving toward those in my life? I soon discovered that holding the tension with love in your heart creates a crucible effect. Everything that is no longer right, rises to the surface until only the essentials remain.

Much to my surprise, it was not only my relationship with the spiritual group that went into the fire, but my relationship with Don as well. The process revealed that which was no longer working between Don and me, too. More distance was required to maintain a loving heart and in 2004 I moved to Los Angeles - alone. Not without irony, I moved back into the neighborhood that I had lived in while working at Disney. There, I held the tension another year while the ultimate course of my marriage came clear.

In the Fall of 2005, I took a long awaited trip to France. It was just what I needed. Like a spring thaw, parts melted away and others blossomed. I discovered a revival of my love of writing. On my return to the States, I made a spontaneous stop in New York where, much to my surprise, I fell in love again. Not with a person but with a city and in an instant I knew my next move.

I then discovered step three in this process of change: courage. *When the way is clear, have the courage to act.* I went back to Los Angeles and set about the task of sorting through everything I owned, deciding what to sell and what to store. Amidst the horror stories people felt compelled to tell me about the high cost of living in New York, I set an intention to find a great apartment in my price range where I could, once again, return to my passion of writing.

I write this as I watch the sun light up the New York skyline from the window of my Upper West Side apartment. I realize that this process of love, purification and courage has yielded results beyond my wildest dreams. Not only has this long and winding road, with all its twists and turns, brought me once again to my original dream of writing in New York City, but something of my true self has been restored as well. Guided by Love and caught in the updraft, I have been gently deposited on the shores of a new world, transported from where I was to where I have always known I would be…and this is just the beginning.

Anna

**Life is not tried,
it is merely survived,
if you're standing outside
the fire.**

Standing Outside the Fire
Garth Brooks and Jenny Yates

Change

True Change

*I*s there a gap between where you are and where you want to be? Is the life you want to live eluding you? Why is it that what we long for in our hearts, and what we experience, seldom match?

We yearn to live passionate and meaningful lives, and yet we cannot seem to break free of our day-to-day responsibilities. We imagine a life that's nourishing and creative, but those dreams are dampened by the need to be realistic and practical.

Instead of creating the world we want, we react to a world that's growing increasingly out of control. We try forcing ourselves into pre-defined roles. Like a square peg in a round hole, we just don't fit. The options at our disposal, are not the options that we want.

This culture we're living in began just a couple of hundred years ago with the birth of the industrial revolution. Work shifted from manual labor to machinery, and agriculture to industry. What had been produced in the home and by small businesses, became mass produced. "Modern conveniences" emerged like the washer, dryer, refrigerator, and vacuum, making life easier. To pay for them, we traded time for money. Now, other people make our clothes and food, even our art and entertainment. We work to pay someone else to do almost everything for us. In some ways, you could say we outsource our lives. We've traded nature for cubicles and time with our families for hours at the office. Emotional depression is at epidemic proportions because we've become disconnected from our own lives. This condition is reflected in the global economy as a financial depression. We've tried to buy our way to happiness, even to the point of spending beyond our means. Still, we're not happy. The jobs and lifestyle options on the menu are no longer appetizing. How then, do we turn this ship around? What course do we set to create a more sustainable world?

To live lives that change us in ways we could never imagine, we must show up where life is happening. That's in the now.

True change, versus change that just re-arranges things, allows Life to have an influence. It allows Life to play a part in what is being created. Life is the *x-factor*. It's what creates the magic, the unexpected. To live lives that surprise us, that change us in ways we could never imagine, that show us options we didn't know existed, we must show up where life is happening and that's *in the now*. This is the same place change happens – in the now. Not yesterday, not tomorrow - *now*.

BEING IN THE MOMENT means being present. We're not dwelling in the past, or we're worrying about the future. We're present, now.

Being in the moment simply means being *present*. It means that we are not distracted by the past or the future. If we're having a conversation with someone, they have our full attention. We're not thinking about where to go for lunch or what we did last night. Whatever we're doing, we are fully present.

All too often, we are anywhere but present. We relive memories from the past and fantasize about what might have been. We worry about things to come, planning strategies and running endless conversations in our heads. We are anywhere but in the *now*.

Moments of crisis become memorable because, just for a moment, we forget everything else, and focus on the *now*. September 11 had that effect. We sat riveted to our televisions, fully present as we witnessed the unfolding events. Before the grief set in, and before we became afraid, there was shock. The known – how far people would go to hurt one another – became the unknown. Now, anything could happen. This resulted in a wave of compassion that spread around the world. That outpouring of love brought us together. That momentary unification carried with it the opportunity to be in agreement and create change based in love.

Fortunately, there are ways besides crises to bring us into the moment. In my own

LOVE is simply an attracting force. It draws us one to another and inexplicably to what we must do or be.

experience of change, I have discovered three actions that, when worked together, help me find my way into the moment and stay there until Life has a chance to work its magic. These three actions allow transformation to occur on purpose and with intent. They are: *love, proximity* and *courage.* Let me explain.

Love

There are many different concepts about love. For our purposes, love is simply an attracting force. It's what we feel a passion for, what energizes and excites us, what brings us joy, and what brings us together in compassion. In short, it draws us one to another and inexplicably to what we must do or be.

I have always loved the way physicist, Brian Swimme, describes love in his book, *The Universe is a Green Dragon*. "Love begins," he says, "when we discover interest. To be interested is to fall in love. To become fascinated is to step into a wild love affair on any level of life." He further explains how each of us has our own unique set of attractions just like atoms and protons. "Destiny unfolds," he concludes, "in the pursuit of individual fascinations and interests."

We turn to love for change because it's the only feeling present in the moment. When we feel sad, we are holding onto the past. Fear is worry about the future, and anger is frustration about both. Love is the only feeling in the here and now. If we want real change in our lives, we must be where change is happening which is in the now. To get to the present moment, we must commit to love.

Proximity

Keeping that loving feeling is usually easier said than done. Resentment, frustration and grief have a way of getting the best of us. To help us remain loving, we have proximity. Proximity means nearness, how close or how far we are to something or someone. When we feel angry with someone, how much distance do we need between us and the other person in order to feel a current of love? Sometimes, walking out of the room and counting to ten is enough. Other times, it may take moving to another country. It may mean detaching emotionally and caring less – or engaging and caring more. Finding the right proximity is key. It allows our hearts to open and our vision to clear. The next step emerges organically motivated by love instead of hindered by fear.

Courage

Courage is required throughout the process of true change. Deciding to change partners, careers, or lifestyles, all take an enormous amount of courage. In that moment, we agree to let go of the familiar and venture into the unknown. It takes courage to stay with the process and

PROXIMITY means nearness, how close or how far we are to something or someone.

not give in to discomfort. Most importantly, it takes courage to act once Life shows us a new direction.

Commit to coming from a place of LOVE

Find your right PROXIMITY and wait for clarity

When the path is clear, have the COURAGE to act.

Working *LOVE*, *PROXIMITY*, and *COURAGE* together ignites change. Possibilities appear where none existed before. If you have the courage to act, you begin a journey to a new and wondrous life.

Here's an example of how *LOVE*, *PROXIMITY*, and *COURAGE* work. A few years ago, I was doing a radio show about living a passionate life. Rachel, a woman in her mid-forties, called in and said, "You can talk all you want about passion, but I don't have that luxury." She described how she worked all day, had two young children, and at night, after feeding and bathing her kids, she had to take care of her sick, elderly parents. This woman felt she had no time for herself because she was too busy with her family obligations.

I'm sure *LOVE* was playing some part in Rachel's motivation to care for her children and parents, but she didn't sound like she was having a very loving experience as we talked. Where's

COURAGE is about taking action.

the love? Where's the joy? Clearly, she loves her family but loving herself is important, also. Becoming aware of her emotions when she's not feeling loving are important. Feelings like resentment, anger, and frustration, are normal and important to acknowledge, too. Being honest with where she is will guide her to where she wants to be.

Next comes *PROXIMITY*. How near or how far does she need to be from her situation to feel loving? When one is in the middle of everything, it's difficult to sort anything out. For Rachel, it might be going out for coffee or taking a night off. Stepping back will help her get in touch with the thoughts going through her head and the feelings running through her heart. Is she doing a lot for others because she feels blessed and wants to give back or is she just afraid to say no? Maybe guilt plays a part. How is she with boundaries? Is she afraid to ask for help?

Having the courage to honestly look at her situation, options appear for Rachel that seemingly weren't there before. Is her husband doing his part? Are there siblings who could help? Does her job pay her what she's worth? Are there community services that could assist her? All that remains is for Rachel to have the *COURAGE* to act.

Igniting Change provides the how-to for implementing *LOVE*, PROXIMITY and COURAGE to change your life. Here's a preview:

- The section on *FIRE* explains how the physics of fire are also at play to ignite change in your life.
- The section on *LOVE* gives a brief history of the coping mechanisms we've developed

to deal with sadness, fear, anger and shame, and how to re-direct those feelings back to love.

- The section on *PROXIMITY* tells us how to build a container that can withstand the pressure of change.

- The section on *COURAGE* explains how to assess the risks of change so we can catch the updraft and fly.

- *Exercises* and *TOOLS* are included to help you integrate the information so your life can start changing in miraculous ways.

How do we bridge the chasm between where we are and where we want to be? Descending the chasm is not an option, but catching an updraft to cross it is. In order to create an updraft, you need heat. To create heat, you need a spark. Are you ready to ignite your life?

Fire

Lessons from the Caveman

*F*or over one million years, humans spent their time refining the arrowhead. Then, about 25,000 years ago we learned how to make a fire and went from

this... to this.

Harnessing the ability to create fire on command brought quantum change for humanity. Until we discovered how to harness fire, we stood in the cold and dark waiting for lightening to strike. When something caught fire, we tended it as if our lives depended on it – which they did.

After fire, we had light and warmth around which to gather. We were able to cook and preserve food, make tools, stave off wild animals, and protect our young. Once we learned how to intentionally ignite fire, we were free to travel about, secure in our ability to have warmth, light, protection, and food. Fire gave us the opportunity to expand our world.

In order to change our lives, we need something as dynamic as fire to transform what we have and expand our possibilities. In this, we are still similar to prehistoric man. We believe that we're subject to our environment. Things happen *to* us. When our experience is bad, we feel cold and miserable, and we struggle to make things better. When life is "good," we tend it for all it's worth because we feel warm and bright. We don't know how adversity happens or when it will strike again, and we hope and pray that our positive experiences will last forever.

As we explore quantum physics, we become less prehistoric in our thinking. We know that our thoughts impact our reality, but for the most part we have yet to master the ability to change our reality with any consistency. We have yet to harness the power of true change – until now. The laws of physics that transform a solid piece of wood into fire are the same laws that transform our lives. Understanding how fire works can help us understand how change works. Let's take a look.

HOW TO BUILD A FIRE

Any good scout can tell you, there are three things you need to build a fire: a spark, fuel, and air.

Spark

The most common way to initiate heat is with friction. You strike a match to a rough surface and, voilà, you have a flame.

Fuel

Apply the flame to a fuel such as wood and let it heat up until it releases its flammable gases.

Air

When wood reaches approximately 500° F, the cellulose in the wood decomposes, and releases flammable gases - namely CH_2O. The carbon, hydrogen, and oxygen atoms are lighter than air,

$$C + H + H + O \qquad \begin{matrix} O \\ O \\ O \end{matrix}$$

and so they begin to rise. Like a magic act, from a seemingly inanimate object like wood, comes movement. Being lighter than the surrounding air, these gases rise, creating an updraft.

The gases meet the oxygen in the air, and a sort of wild party takes place called a chain reaction.

$$C+H+H+O \quad \begin{matrix} O \\ O \end{matrix} \qquad C+O+O \quad H+H+O$$

The hydrogen and oxygen are very attracted to one another and so they change partners becoming water vapor ($H2O$) and carbon dioxide ($CO2$). This process continues as long as there's fuel to feed it. The speed with which this exchange takes place is so rapid that the mere process of the exchange produces energy and light. We begin with a spark, allow things to heat up, transform into something else, and rise. Hummm…. How could we use this technology to move from where we are to where we want to be?

How to build a fire

Spark   *We use friction to create a spark*

Fuel   *The spark heats up the fuel.*

Ash   *The hot fuel releases gases that mix with the air.*

Produces:

Light   *The rapid speed of carbon drawn to oxygen creates light.*

Energy   *Energy is freed up as old structures are released.*

Air   *All that remains is ash.*

HOW TO BUILD A FIRE IN YOUR LIFE

We've looked at how change works in science. Now let's see how it works with us.

Realization is the Spark

First we need friction to make a spark. Friction is produced by two things rubbing against each other. It's anything that makes us feel uncomfortable and compels us to change, anything that's not working in our lives.

The spark is the aha that comes when we realize something needs to change. It's the light bulb going on in your head that tells you things are not how they should be.

Your Situation is the Fuel

Next, we need fuel. Fuel is our day-to-day situations. It's waking up next to your unaffectionate spouse, going to work and having to deal with that difficult co-worker, being reminded of someone you love who's passed away, or seeing the clutter you can't seem to eliminate. It may be the bills that just pile up, the weight you just can't seem to lose, or going to bed alone, again. The fuel you have to work with is a situation that has suddenly become untenable.

The situation naturally starts heating up because of your awareness that you are no longer content with your life as it currently is. You go to work and you're hyperaware of your boss' unacceptable behavior, or you come home and can't stand the mess another minute. We could equate the flammable gases released from wood to the thoughts and feelings that arise from the changing situations in our lives. As soon as we become aware of what needs to change, we suddenly become more aware of how we feel and what we think about our circumstances.

Life is the Air

When wood hits the right temperature, the gases break free of their dense form. Because they're lighter than air, they rise. Only then are they free to become something else. They change when they're exposed to something more attractive – oxygen.

In our lives, the final step is for our thoughts and feelings to be exposed to something more attractive like oxygen. We might call this *Life*. Without air or oxygen, we cease to exist. Without life we're dead. Since Life is invisible to us, we could also describe it as *the mystery* or *the unexpected*. This universal force runs through us. It has been spoken of poetically as *the breath that animates us*. A simple way of connecting with Life is to look out through your eyes and ask yourself: *Who is looking?*

As we merge with Life, we become the *observer*. We observe our thoughts and feelings rather than react to them. The observer operates beyond the mind. It's the x-factor we need to take us

> **Since LIFE is invisible to us, we could describe it as the mystery or the unexpected. This universal force runs through us and has been poetically spoken of as the breath that animates us.**

beyond what we know, into the unknown. Like oxygen acting on CH_2O, we observe our thoughts and feelings, and they grow and change. Let's see what happens when we plug Life into our equation:

- The spark is the realization that something wants to change in our lives.
- Things heat up as we interact with the situation.
- This brings up thoughts and feelings.
- Observing our thoughts and feelings allows them to relax and change.

New Results

During the process of our molecules re-partnering, something else happens. Something new is produced. Creating a fire with wood produces LIGHT, ENERGY, and ASH. Igniting our personal process results in GROWTH, PASSION, and RELEASE.

When you shine a light onto something, you dispel the darkness and create awareness. You're able to see something that you couldn't see before. The result is growth.

In fire, breaking the old chemical bond releases energy. When we allow our old ways of thinking and feeling to come into alignment with Life, the old patterns are broken and energy is freed up. We lighten up and have more energy for change. In this way, we reclaim our passion.

Ash is the final product that's produced in a fire. At the personal level, as we stand in the Fire of Truth, we release old patterns and allow them to burn away. Like the Phoenix rising from the ashes, we take with us new insights and the passion to move forward. We leave behind the ash, which can be equated to our outmoded thoughts and beliefs, or a situation we leave behind that no longer applies. We release it and move on.

Fire is a transformative event. It's the process of molecules regrouping and becoming something new. Likewise, change is the process of transforming our current experiences into new possibilities. It's a way of elevating our lives to a whole new level. This is the alchemical experience we need if we want to truly change our lives.

Learning how to harness fire took us from arrowheads to space travel in a mere 25,000 years. Awakening to the forces at work in our lives is the equivalent of coming out of the Dark Ages. It has the magnitude of being able to strike a match and start a fire. Once again, the control is in our hands.

How to build a fire in your life

Spark

THE AHA!
You get it. Where there's friction,
something needs to change.

Fuel

THE SITUATION
The daily friction causes thoughts and
feelings to arise

Air

THE OBSERVER
Detached, you observe your reactions,
keeping what's relevant and letting go of
the rest.

Produces change:

Light

AWARENESS
Seeing clearly, we glimpse new
possibilities.

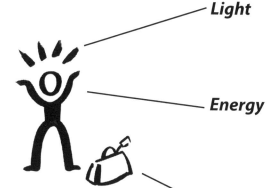

Energy

MOVEMENT
Movement is created by energy freed up
from letting go.

Ash

RELEASE.
Letting go gets rid of the old "baggage".

TENDING THE FIRE OF CHANGE

Our primitive ancestors discovered that fire not only kept them warm, but it gave them a better quality of life. It drew them together, creating families and community. It helped them evolve and grow. They understood the importance of keeping the flame alive.

This same care and tending is required to keep our hopes and dreams alive, to keep the fire burning within. No doubt we have an ample supply of friction and fuel to power change. So why aren't things just transforming? The reason is because we haven't been thinking in terms of *stewarding* the fire.

In order to participate in change and allow our lives to be transformed, we must learn how to become fire-keepers.

In reality, we rarely take time to tend the transformational process that is taking place in our lives. We run around putting out fires or desperately trying to fan the embers of our dreams, keeping most of our focus on the immediate tasks at hand. Meanwhile, we may occasionally notice a niggling feeling somewhere in the background. It might be sadness or depression, frustration, anger, or even rage. But the physical work must get done and so we stifle these feelings. Only in stolen moments do we indulge in contemplation.

What has been lacking is our knowledge of how to create a crucible and keep the fire burning until the process is complete. In order to participate in change and allow our lives to be transformed, we must learn how to become fire-keepers. We must learn how to set the container, get the fire burning, and keep it burning until the process is complete.

True change occurs through an intense internal fire that burns away what we no longer need. A re-made self arises from the ashes. In order to harness change, we must learn how to steward such a mystical fire.

Love

Commit to coming from a place of LOVE

Find your right PROXIMITY and wait for clarity

When the path is clear, have the COURAGE to act.

Into the Now

In the present moment, there is a weaving together of experiences. Love – wholeness – source – consciousness. Experience any one of them, and we experience them all. Unconditional love is just another way of describing what is happening in the *Now*.

When we experience love, we are in the moment. We cannot be there and feel anything else. If we're in grief, we're in the past. If we're in fear, we're in the future. Love has various faces, including but not limited to joy and compassion. When we experience love, we feel connected and whole. All at once, we're one with the source of all life. We are conscious and aware when we are in that place. Everything that has ever been and ever will be is present in that moment.

The ills of the world can be healed from such a place. Relying on conditions of the past to determine right action in the present will not work. Plotting in anticipation of the future will not help us determine what needs to happen next. Only in the moment – connected by love, free of illusion, and sourced by Life – can we transform our reality. Visible and invisible find a meeting place within us. Rooted in this place of truth, our vision begins to clear. What is *real* separates from the *unreal*. Defense mechanisms are disarmed. Judgment, anger, criticism, and blame show themselves for what they are: a reflection of our internal state. What seemed impossible to fix, becomes the path of transformation.

Exercise

Change only happens in the now. Here is a quick way of identifying where you are and getting back to the moment.

PAST   FUTURE

NOW

If you're feeling depressed, it may be that your energy is snagged in the past. Relative to the present moment, you're behind. You need to get moving! Get out. Walk. Call a friend. Do something, anything!

If your worried or nervous, you're trying to think ahead so you'll be safe, so everything will be okay. Though it seems like the only option is to DO MORE, on the time scale you're ahead. In order to get back into the moment, you need to slow down! That might seem counterproductive when there's a lot to do, but you will be much more productive and able to think more clearly if you slow it down.

LOVE IS A COMPASS

By setting our course for love, we are guided back to wholeness. Expressing love, we are on track and homeward bound. Any other emotion alerts us to the fact that we've veered off course and are in need of a course correction.

From this perspective, we can be thankful for pain, because it warns us that we have disconnected from something we love, something we desire to reconnect with. If we allow ourselves to be vulnerable to pain, it can guide us back to love. We set our ego aside in exchange for love. When we welcome love into our hearts and extend love from our hearts, our world expands. Resist and we enter a downward spiral.

If we allow ourselves to be vulnerable to pain, it can guide us back to love.

Love is a process involving the heart and mind. It only resides in hearts and minds free of judgment and blame. As we enter a commitment to come from a place of love in relation to a situation or person in our lives, we must become aware of what we are feeling and thinking. What do you want to play host to? It's *your* body, *your* heart, and *your* mind. Harboring feelings such as anger, resentment, or shame are unhealthy to your well-being. Like a garden, what do you want to grow inside of you? Do you want a creative, light-filled atmosphere or something dark and negative? We choose in every moment. We must learn to re-sensitize ourselves to our feelings and become more aware of what's moving through our minds.

Love binds the universe together. It's the attracting force that draws us one to another and back to wholeness. We either allow ourselves to be drawn by love or we resist it. Feelings such as anger, sadness, greed, or shame merely indicate that we are pushing love away and with it our hopes and dreams.

This process of coming from a place of love puts us in the path of Life.

This process of *coming from a place of love* puts us in the path of Life. Once on the path of Life, we are in a position to allow clarification to occur. At that point, the obstacles that have impeded our way arise for us to see.

There are many triggers that can hamper our path in this regard. In an attempt to survive painful experiences, we develop coping mechanisms meant to protect us from pain. These self-erected walls become our prisons. We must re-learn how to access our thoughts and feelings, how to disable our coping mechanisms, and disarm the triggers.

We begin this journey by doing a quick review of where we've been and how we got there. We'll take a look at how some of our coping mechanisms were created in the first place so we can better understand how to remove them.

A BRIEF HISTORY

We're born whole

We can learn about our true state of being by looking at babies. They're whole and perfect. My family could sit around for hours – make that *has* sat around for hours – watching the new baby in the family, every gesture, every coo. We're drawn to them. We want to hold them and be close to them because they carry a purity about them. They're like little balls of love. Babies are also very much in the moment. All they know is: *I'm hungry now. I need sleep now.* They are a great example of love in the present moment.

We're introduced to the world of separation

If all goes well in the womb, our needs are met. We have warmth and shelter, food and love. It's *fluid.* There is no differentiation between the need and the provision. It all flows as one. It's Life and it's in perfect order. We enter the world expecting unconditional love. Instead, we're introduced to the world of separation. Even with the best intentions of our parents, we have needs that aren't met. We're hungry, but we don't get fed. We're wet, but we don't get changed. We hurt, and no one understands. This lack becomes a need unmet, a longing unfulfilled.

We start taking notes

Cliff Barry, who created a personal development process called Shadow Work®, can often be heard saying, "We will love joyfully or painfully, but love we will." To love and be loved is human. It's who we are. We need love to survive. Children have a natural instinct for what works and what does not work in order to ensure a connection with others. In working with people who have had troubled childhoods, it never ceases to amaze me how resilient they are. They behave in all kinds of ways to avoid trouble and eke out even the slightest affection.

In dysfunctional homes, children become very creative in knowing what will and what will not set off their parents. They quickly learn how to become invisible in order to avoid a violent parent's wrath. Incest, alcoholism, drug addiction, and emotional irregularities exist in our world – and beautiful, whole children must adapt to survive. We learn how to follow suit and walk in separation with the rest of the population.

All of these learned behaviors take their toll because they teach us that this is how to love. Love is a learned behavior, and our parents or guardians are our teachers. It isn't until we get older that we realize we can re-educate ourselves.

We Adapt

Children go off to school, where they are educated as to what is and isn't socially acceptable – usually by shame. Even the word *shame* can make us feel uncomfortable. We could say that shame is simply something we've been told doesn't fit into society. It could be described as something that might require forgiveness from oneself or another. Either way, shame ensures separation. We put a veil between us and the shameful experience, and we rarely want to revisit it. If it's bad enough, we build walls around it and throw away the key.

We become socialized at a young age. We learn what fits in and what results in harassment and criticism. Who we are is soon being shaped by what fits in. If there are people on hand who encourage the parts of ourselves that are different, these parts can survive and become our strengths. If not, they go into shadow – the good parts as well as the bad. Without the caring eye of a parent, teacher, or mentor, we often find our way to mainstream and mediocrity when, in reality, we were born to be uniquely great.

This is where we begin muting who we are. It's more important to survive and fit in than to stand out and excel. We learn how to translate our feelings into acceptable messages. We narrow the band.

The parts of us that are sent into isolation may be negative or positive. It could be our creative nature, our joy or our humor. I remember watching home movies when I was a kid. There I was, larger than life, dancing across the screen, obviously having the time of my life! But then someone called me a show off and said I was hogging all the attention. They may have only been kidding, but I was so ashamed, I hid away a part of my free spirit that day.

Parts of us that we need are often wrapped up in the parts of ourselves that we deny, good or bad. Often we quarantine those parts because we've only experienced them in hurtful ways. In a sense, we throw the baby out with the bathwater.

In its purest form, anger, for example, gives us the energy for change. If we deny our anger, we often lose our power as well. We cease to be able to adequately defend ourselves or have the passion to power change. This is true not only of anger, but of other emotions as well. Mixed together are our natural urges, talents and the emotions that guide us. All of these are essential to our well-being and the full expression of who we are.

When we stuff the parts of ourselves that might get us into trouble into a metaphorical bag, we often cause even more trouble. As a middle child, I learned at an early age that stealing the limelight from my older sister came with a price to pay, so I opted to be "quiet and smart."

The problem is that each time we disown a part of ourselves, we have to tell ourselves a story about where it went. I told myself "shining" is embarrassing and "reserved" is smart. I began to seek out role models to substantiate this new guideline. I turned to career women in movies. They were tough and smart. Yes, I would be like them.

These stories become our personalities. The ego is the story-keeper. Its job is to keep track of our fabricated truths so we can keep our stories straight. This is an important job. Remember,

> **The EGO is the story-keeper. Its job is to keep track of our fabricated truths so we can keep our stories straight.**

these stories were created for our very survival. This is how our personalized world of illusions is constructed and maintained. We assess our world through tales we are no longer conscious of and make blind choices that create our reality. The good and bad news is that nothing stays stuffed away forever. It leaks out. That which we vow never to do or to be almost always finds its way into expression.

We Project

Robert Bly, who spoke about stuffing parts of ourselves into a bag in his book, *A Little Book on the Human Shadow*, says that if we stuff things in hard enough, they come 360 degrees around the world and show up in the person across from us. This is popularly known as *projection*. If you want to know what's hidden in your bag, look at what irritates you about other people, and also what you envy or admire.

We project disowned parts of our psyche onto those around us such as our friends, lovers, and bosses. Rather than recognize these lost parts of ourselves and reclaim them, we try to stuff *that* person's expression, too. For example, now, when I see someone else shining, an unconscious link connects it to "embarrassing." My instinct is to distance myself from shining, and so I negate that person's expression and push them away. This is a nice way of saying that I criticize or judge them. Unfortunately, we go through life casting people around us to play the roles of our unfinished past.

Relationships are the epitome of projection. Harville Hendricks popularized the term *imago* in his book *Getting the Love You Want*. The imago is a profile we create of all the unfinished business we have with our parents and other early caregivers. The imago is created from the ways our needs for love were met or unmet, which, in turn, shapes the parts of ourselves we express and suppress. We eventually find a partner who embodies all of the unexpressed parts of ourselves – hence the expression: opposites attract.

At first we adore our new partner. They are the embodiment of all our lost parts and we feel free at last! The minute the relationship becomes committed, the first order of business is to stifle those traits. It's okay to have them *out there*, but we have learned the hard way that they're unsafe *in here*. Once the relationship becomes intimate and the two worlds merge, control must be applied. Over time, the very things we found ourselves attracted to become liabilities in the relationship.

For the most part, we are unaware that all of this is going on. It happens at a subconscious level. Regardless, this learned behavior dictates our actions all day long, every day of our lives. It becomes apparent that until we become conscious of the script running behind the scenes, we are no more than puppets in the drama.

A vivid example of this happened for me one day when a boyfriend and I were shopping at a hardware store. Without saying anything, he wandered off to look for something. This might have been insignificant to someone else, but it triggered an intense reaction in me. My first flush was a painful sense of abandonment, which I quickly covered with anger. *How dare he just disappear? Doesn't he want to be with me? What kind of person just walks away without saying something?*

It was fairly obvious after I'd stormed out of the store and sat crying in the car that perhaps this was a bit of an overreaction to the present situation. The drama escalated to operatic proportions when my boyfriend found me in the car hysterical. He was taken by surprise, to say the least, when he realized that he was in trouble for going off to find a rake. This, in turn, triggered the underlying pattern he got from his mother, which said: *I just can't please you.*

Later, as I allowed myself to calm down and experience my pain, I realized that his walking away had triggered the memory of losing love and attention in childhood. I had carried my unfulfilled needs over into my relationship and overlaid it onto my partner.

We Perpetuate

While we're in our illusions reliving the past or worrying about the future, nobody's home! We are not present in the moment where life is happening, even though we can effect change only in the moment. Without living consciously in the present, we are doomed to wallow in our pain and misery, remaining unaware of the fact that it's not even real. It's like trying to find our way out of a dream from which the only way out is to wake up.

We mold ourselves to a wounded world. We inherit a society created by people adapting to other people's wounds. Better to play it safe than to be sorry. If you play this out, you can begin to understand the world in which we live. Cautious choices lead to fewer options.

How do we break free of this hereditary trap? Can we, in fact, rise above the miasma and see with clarity? When we react unconsciously, we perpetuate an unreal world. But when we get control of our subconscious, our impulses no longer control us. We begin to make powerful changes that result in something new and real. This is the *awakening* spiritual teachers have been pointing us to for eons – acting from an awakened state, living in the real world. It is only in an awakened state that we truly *live*. Everything else is sleepwalking.

I find it interesting that Leonardo DiVinci, whose ideas are considered genius, took to writing in what appears to the rest of us as mirror-image handwriting – backwards and to the left. It's almost as if he stepped through the mirror, and from that point on he saw and wrote things opposite to the rest of the world.

Basing our choices in fear rather than love, almost everything we create is the opposite of what we want.

We have been occupying an unreal state, a house of mirrors. We are fooling ourselves into believing that we are *living,* when, in fact, we resist Life. We accept it in measured doses. Basing our choices in fear rather than love, almost everything we create is the opposite of what we want. *I am afraid of being abandoned so I cling to my partner. In the end, my clinging drives him away and I am abandoned.* What we long for is connection. What we get is separation.

For untold generations, our world has been built upon choices based in protection and fear. We hedge our bets and minimize risks. It's worked, of course. We're still here. With each generation, however, we narrow the possibilities.

It's clear we've wandered off course. If we are to find our way back to wholeness, we must dispel the illusions and see things for what they truly are. We must find a way to discern the real from the unreal. One way of doing this is *love*.

RE-SENSITIZING TO LOVE

There are many intangible things we can theorize about. Heaven, hell, and even the nature of God. But there is one thing we can be certain is real and that is love. We know love exists because we can give or receive it anytime we choose. You could say it's omnipresent.

Love is like true north on a compass. Aiming for it leads us to center. It guides us back to wholeness. Any other emotion alerts us to the fact that we have veered off course and are in need of a course correction. We are on a detour and taking the long way home.

Within this context, discomfort and pain become our allies. They warn us that we have disconnected from love. Allow ourselves to listen to the pain and it will guide us back to

Exercise

Knowing your personal journey can help you better understand your reaction to your life. Recognizing what may have caused you to bury feelings and alter thoughts, allows you to reconnect with more authentic emotions and ideas.

Take a piece of paper and draw a wavy line around it like a winding path. This is your life so far. At one end of the line, write: BIRTH. At the other end, write: NOW. Along the line, briefly note all of the pivotal events and your age at that time. Include situations that made a significant impact, any particularly happy, sad, fearful, or angry times. Note any crossroads. What choice did you make?

When you're finished, step back as if you were observing this person's life from above. Starting with early childhood, what patterns might have been set in place? Who had a primary influence? Where do those patterns repeat themselves later in life and who played the roles? What trends do you see? What happened at the crossroads? What did you choose? What did you want to choose? What stopped you?

Now that you can see the patterns, things can change. Be aware over the next few days of how these historical patterns might be showing up in your life now.

wholeness.

Our feelings are a built-in guidance system. Like so many other things, however, we've gotten it backwards. Instead of embracing our feelings and following their guidance, we resist them to the point of rendering them almost imperceptible.

In his book *Nonviolent Communication: A Language of Life,* author Marshall Rosenberg invites us to familiarize ourselves with the language of the feeling realm. He provides a list of almost 275 words to describe a wide range of feelings. Rosenberg suggests, "By developing a vocabulary of feelings that allows us to clearly and specifically name or identify our emotions, we can connect more easily with one another. Allowing ourselves to be vulnerable by expressing our feelings can help resolve conflicts."

The more in touch we are with our feelings, the more conscious we are of our experience. Rather than reacting unconsciously because of some imperceptible urge, we become aware of the feeling and have a choice of what to do about it. There is a difference between *being* angry and knowing we *feel* angry. One is a reaction, the other is being in the present. The moment we become aware that we feel angry, we are present in that moment. Being present, we have the opportunity to truly change our situation rather than just repeat old ways.

EDGE

One day while I was exercising, I noticed that as I stretched I would hit a place of discomfort and then stop. The response was purely involuntarily. I would feel a slight pain, perhaps try a bit more, and then accept this as my limit and stop. I realized I had just encountered an invisible *edge.*

Later, I began to observe this edge in other aspects of my life as well. I realized that I had emotional edges, too. I watched myself reach subtle levels of discomfort in conversations and remove myself from the situation as quickly as possible.

I saw mental edges, too. In a heart-to-heart conversation one day with my brother, he gave me a great gift by helping me see a belief I was holding that I used like a sword to keep people at bay. I was using my beliefs to protect my vulnerability, but in the end they kept me separated.

These edges are often born out of our early life experiences. They are the borders of our unfinished business. Over time, these physical, emotional, and mental limits define who we are. They establish our invisible boundaries in the world. We tell ourselves: *I have a fear of flying so I avoid travel. I don't want to be in the same room with my ex-husband so I stay away from family gatherings. I see a person I have a conflict with and go out of my way to avoid seeing them. I have been hurt in relationships so I am alone.* Instead of these feelings just being a reaction to a situation, they begin to define us and the choices we make, ultimately defining our lives.

Whether we're aware of these invisible edges or not, the thoughts and feelings begin to define a comfort zone. We stay within a defined perimeter, never going beyond. We feel the pain and react. We hit the wall and retreat. The more pain, the smaller the box we retreat into.

For the most part, we go through life, unaware that what silently controls our emotions is an individualized matrix of past experiences. We're influenced by our upbringing, the culture in which we're raised, the religion we're taught, and the country in which we live. We might have beliefs about what we're good at and what we're not. We might tell ourselves: *My sister's the pretty one. I'm the smart one. Or my brother's the successful one. I'm the creative one.* But is that who we *really* are? If we are conscious of the thoughts and feelings arising, our own awareness effects the change. Our awareness, the part that looks out through our eyes, becomes the catalyst for transformation. The opportunity is to awaken from this state of unconsciousness and stay awake. All too often, however, we are numb to the pain and, consequently, numb to the very thing that could guide us out of pain.

We must be willing to embrace the unknown. In this way, Life becomes interesting again.

These invisible edges go along dictating the course of our lives, unless we go beyond them. *LOVE, PROXIMITY* and *COURAGE* are a way of recognizing and moving through the edge. By re-sensitizing to our thoughts and feelings, we become aware that we have hit an edge. Once we know we've hit the outer perimeter, we have the choice of going through it.

Here is a final thought about the edge. It usually feels the worst just before we go through

Exercise

PART 1; Here is a simple exercise for you to have an experience of edge.

Stand up. Bend at the waist like you're going to touch your toes. Bend to the point where you would feel inclined to stop. When you hit that spot, feel the ache or the discomfort. This is your physical edge.

Now, inhaling, shift your attention to the life flowing through your body on the inside. As you exhale, be the life flowing through the discomfort. See if you can experience your body relaxing and stretching through the edge.

Most people who excel at something have learned to go through their edges, to transcend the pain and keep going. When we hit an edge, it's actually a signal that we've reached an opportunity for growth. Time to stay focused and go through it!

PART 2; Think of something in your life you feel uncomfortable with. It might be something you feel pressure about, something you're having difficulty with, or something that's upsetting to you. Write it down. Ask yourself: What am I afraid of? What am I unwilling to let go of? What am I unwilling to do? What is the opportunity here? What would my life be like if I go through this edge? What will change? What will I have that I don't have now?

it. Our freedom lies just beyond the point at which we believe we cannot go any further. In fact, we stand at the threshold of a new life. Too often, we set up camp at the doorway. We park along the side of the road, unpack and get comfortable rather than pushing on.

The words of my former neighbor in Austin, Texas come to mind. He was giving us driving directions to get out of the state and he kept saying in his Texas drawl, "Now when you get to El Paso, you just keep on goin'." Delivering a bit more information, he would then reiterate, "Now, remember. When you get to El Paso, don't stop. You just keep on goin'." This is similar to what I would say to you. "When you get to the edge, just keep on going. Don't stop. Just keep on going all the way through. It may feel painful for awhile, but that just means you're almost there!"

Our job is to become explorers, to recognize the edge and go beyond. We must be willing to embrace the unknown. In this way, Life becomes interesting again. It becomes an adventure. Re-sensitizing to our feelings, we reclaim control of our reactions and, subsequently, our lives. In this we discover real power and know true freedom.

Proximity

Commit to coming from a place of LOVE

Find your right PROXIMITY and wait for clarity

When the path is clear, have the COURAGE to act.

Creating a Container for Change

*T*he word *proximity* means nearness: How close or how far do you need to be to a situation or person to keep a current of love in your heart? Remember, love keeps us in the moment, aligned with truth. By adjusting our proximity, we can raise or lower the intensity. The higher the heat, the more thoughts and feelings arise. When we reach the point of overwhelm, we take a step back until we can, once again, process what's moving through us.

PROXIMITY works a lot like a camera. It gives us the ability to bring things into sharper focus by zooming in or out. We use *PROXIMITY* to help us gain a clearer perspective. If we're embroiled in a situation that's quite heated, it can be difficult to see clearly. Backing up allows us to perceive accurately and make a healthy decision. Likewise, too much distance between us and something we care about can make it difficult to connect. Sometimes adjusting our proximity means moving in closer so we can take in more detail.

PROXIMITY helps us gain perspective. It allows us to see our lives in focus. The more practiced we become, the more graceful our dance with Life. *PROXIMITY* also allows our thoughts and feelings to come up at a manageable rate so we can learn about ourselves and grow without becoming overwhelmed. Ultimately, *PROXIMITY* is about helping us see the truth so we can make choices based on truth and love, rather than fear or anger. Love-based choices are always sustainable and carry us to the next level, whereas choices based in fear, anger, or sadness tend to create more of the same and also more pain.

ADJUSTING PROXIMITY

We can adjust our proximity both externally and internally. Externally, it's a matter of distance and involvement. People who have painful relationships with family sometimes move far away. This allows them distance to gain perspective on their lives so healing can occur. People having marital problems sometimes turn to separation as a way of creating distance in order to gain a clearer picture of what needs to happen next.

If you're unable to create physical distance, there is always internal control. We have the choice to engage or detach emotionally and mentally to varying degrees. Maybe we've been holding back and need to let our guard down and be more vulnerable. Or maybe we need to let go. One of the reasons we cling is because we believe that the person or situation has something we need that we cannot provide for ourselves. This can make us co-dependent. In this case, we're too close. By stepping back and detaching emotionally, even for a moment, we give ourselves a chance to see other options.

Here's an example of *PROXIMITY* in action. Phil, a client of mine, was in a job he hated. His boss exhibited tyrannical behavior and made Phil's life miserable on a daily basis. Phil has four children, and was not at liberty to just quit his job. Needless to say, he was feeling stressed.

Trapped in a miserable job and unable to give voice to his frustration, he began to internalize his unhappiness and eventually became ill. We began to talk about *PROXIMITY* and the importance of distancing himself from his job so he could gain perspective. No matter how much I assured him that there was a way through his dilemma, trust was a leap of faith he was unwilling to take.

Finally, I said, "I know you don't believe you have any options, but would you even consider being open to the possibility that something could change?" At last, he yielded. "Yes," he said. "I would." I wrote this thought on a piece of paper: "I am open to the possibility that something can change." Then I instructed him to place this statement on his bathroom mirror, where he would see it every day.

"I am open to the possibility that things can change."

His illness led to a short leave of absence. During the time away from his job, and in closer proximity to his family, his values began to re-prioritize. He began to re-evaluate what was important to him. Phil realized that his family and his health were more important than his job and that without his health he was of little use to anyone.

On his first day back to work, he was, once again, under attack. He tried to follow his old pattern of stuffing his feelings, but he had a new awareness of the toll this could take on his health. Instead, Phil did something completely new and different. Rather than act while he was angry, he left his office and went outside to sit quietly. He breathed and waited for his emotions to settle down.

Before long, his vision began to clear. He finally saw the big picture. He realized that he was no longer willing to sacrifice himself for the good of the whole. This was Phil's "moment of truth." He was faced with the leap of faith he had been desperately trying to avoid.

> ### This is the hero's journey:
> ### knowing what we must do,
> ### while having no idea of the outcome.

This is the hero's journey: knowing what we must do, while having no idea of the outcome. Ask anyone in a similar position and they will tell you that it's not so much about courage as it is no longer being able to live with the lie or the pain. It's about allowing ourselves to be guided by something greater than fear – love. In Phil's case, it was love for himself, his family, and Life.

Phil proceeded to the human resources department and told them that his job was not a fit. He made it clear that he was no longer willing to subject himself to the conditions under which he had been working.

He went home that night with no idea about what might happen next. He knew only that he had honored his personal truth. He knew that whatever happened next was, in a sense, out of his control. He had elected to dance with the mystery, and what unfolded would, no doubt, be a surprise.

Indeed, it was a surprise. The next day, Phil received a phone call informing him that not only had his boss been fired, but Phil was being offered his boss' job. Apparently, there had been several other serious complaints filed against his supervisor. Needless to say, Phil was shocked – not only because he was offered a new job, but because the process of being in his truth had actually worked.

Phil has more faith now in the handwritten note posted on his mirror: "I am open to the possibility that things can change." Believing in Life was the leap of faith he had been afraid to take. It was, in fact, the leap of faith he hadn't even believed existed. As a result, he is now in a position to create a positive work environment that benefits not only himself and his family, but all of the other people who work with him as well. Love expands and multiplies. Fear contracts.

PRESSURE

Pressure plays a vital role in change. When I was a child, my father – who is an engineer and fascinated with how things work – was always trying to get one of the kids to ask for a steam engine for Christmas. He would describe in detail how you get the engine going, and then you hook things up to it, and it powers other things. "Don't you want that?" he would ask. "No," we would repeatedly answer. Instead we would opt for dolls and bikes.

Because of my father's fascination with the steam engine, I have a moderate understanding about pressure. When molecules heat up, they expand. If they're in a container, like a steam engine, their expansion creates pressure. You can use that pressure to create movement.

Managing Pressure

One of my spiritual teachers used to talk about pressure and transformation. He would say that we should welcome pressure because it creates movement. He told us how we, too, have a container within that's designed to withstand pressure. That container is our inner strength, our ability to stay with the process. He urged us to learn to be strong, hold steady and to avoid creating leaks in the container by "blowing out".

PROXIMITY assists us in keeping the pressure at manageable levels so change can occur. Finding our right place in relationship to a situation becomes a dance we do with Life. How near or how far do we need to be to keep a current of love or peace or well-being in our hearts? If we feel overwhelmed, we can step back. If we feel numb, we can step in.

> **The CONTAINER is our inner strength, our ability to stay with the process.**

Exercise

What's wanting to change in your life? Where's the friction? Write it down.

Now, ask yourself: Am I willing to allow this situation to change? What often comes up at this point is, "Yes, but I don't know how." We only need to know what. The how is up to Life.

Write an affirmation: I'm open to the possibility that _____ can change.

Congratulations. You've just created a container for change.

New beginnings are a delicate time. When things are new, we need to protect them. Like a baby in the womb, we take care to ensure the baby's development before exposing it to the world. When the development is complete and the baby is ready to enter the world, the pressure of contractions comes to push the newborn out.

How near or far do we need to be from a person or situation, to keep a current of love in our hearts?

It's the same in any creative process. We must take care during the early stages. I have always loved the process of building a campfire. First and foremost, there is the vital step of setting the fire ring. Next comes a pleasant stroll to round up the ingredients - dry pine needles and twigs, armfuls of thin branches, and the logs.

There is the delicate piling of the needles just so, to allow for air to get through. You pile the twigs in an A-frame arcing over the needles, then the branches, and finally the logs. Next is the moment of setting match to kindling. You wait with anticipation to see if the twigs will catch. You protect it from the wind. Too much will blow the whole thing out, too little and it will die. You protect it and fan it. Finally, the twigs catch, igniting the branches and then, with more stoking, the logs join in. So many things can happen along the way, but taking care, you soon have a place of warmth and light to share with others.

Likewise, exposing a new idea too soon may destroy it. Sharon was a successful accountant in a metropolitan city for twenty years. Growing tired of the daily grind, she began to consider what else she might do. Sharon looked at the row of books on her bookshelf about bed and breakfasts and decided maybe the time had come to pursue her dream of opening a B&B.

Without thinking, she casually mentioned her idea in the break room the next day at work. Not surprisingly, it was met with casual and thoughtless comments like, "You'd be bored out of your mind in the country," and "You need to be a people person to run a B&B."

That night, somewhat discouraged, Sharon called a close friend and told her she wanted to talk about something important to her and asked for her friend's attention, which she got. She then shared her idea. Knowing of Sharon's love of cooking and entertaining, and also knowing of Sharon's waning interest in her accounting job, this trusted friend encouraged Sharon to keep the dream alive.

Over the next few months, Sharon took great pleasure in researching locations, creating a business plan, and setting a timeline. One by one, she began to include others – the realtor who caught her vision, the owner of the B&B she loved staying at, a friend who wanted to invest. They became a part of the foundation of her dream as it began to solidify in the world.

Now, much more prepared to include an outer ring of feedback, Sharon met with the owner of the accounting firm. She informed him of her plan which now included a departure date. In addition to sharing a bit of her plans, she thanked him for twenty years of employment and confirmed her commitment to helping him find a suitable replacement. In turn, he acknowledged her commitment to his company over the years, admitted he would miss her, but lent his support to her new endeavor.

Sharon then shared her plans one-on-one with those closest to her at work, garnering support and well-wishes from them. She then let the "grapevine" do the rest. By now, her own sense of commitment to the project was solidified with a buffer of support around her making her plans unshakeable.

After learning the hard way in the break room, Sharon applied the principle of *PROXIMITY* to each step of her plan, keeping the pressure to a manageable level that supported the growth of her dream. She allowed her own substance also known as confidence, knowledge and preparedness to build before taking it to the next level, rather than be overwhelmed by careless feedback.

As with building a fire, it is essential to contain the fire of transformative change. We do this by being intentional. This creates the invisible *container* that holds all of the experiences that follow. Sharon began her process in the break room without setting her container. She shared something precious to her without much thought or intention. The result? A wildfire. After that, a wiser Sharon selected who she shared with, and how she shared with them. She was intentional. She did it on purpose.

This doesn't mean that you're always going to get the response you want. Exposing your idea is like placing it in the refining fire. You may get challenging feedback. For example, Sharon's boss might not have been so gracious. Doubts and fears are bound to come up. Other people projecting their own fear and doubt on you. It's all good. Someone may be showing you a piece you hadn't thought of. Consider it all, make adjustments if necessary, and then discard the rest. With each pass through the fire, your dream becomes stronger and brighter.

If you're lucky, you may have supportive parents who cheer you on. Sometimes, however, a parent's support is tainted by his or her own failure and disappointment. Without meaning to, they may impose their own fears and discouragement onto the next generation.

Many people have a reluctance to move beyond their family's level of success. I've seen it many times with my clients. Somehow they view it as a betrayal if they surpass their father's or mother's accomplishments or move out of the family's social status. Ironically, if they're willing to change and live up to their personal vision, it can infuse the entire family with hope.

HOLDING THE CONTAINER

We may feel uncomfortable or afraid as pressure builds and try to release it. This is understandable. It can be intense! Unless we are used to this type of experience, we will, most likely, do just about anything to avoid the discomfort. In other words, we try to break open the container and let off steam.

Fortunately, or unfortunately, our culture is filled with opportunities for distraction. Shopping, drinking, watching television, surfing the Internet, and sleeping are just a few. We each have our own way of escaping discomfort.

In our lives, the pressure comes through daily situations, such as money, relationships, and children. It's up to us to maintain our inner container so the fire becomes hot enough to burn away all but what's real. Painful as it may be, once we can see things for what they are, they can

If we constantly break the cycle that's trying to build, we remain exactly where we are. There is no movement.

change. We may have to get through a lot of subterfuge from the point of knowing something needs to change to the point of gaining clarity. At each step, we may be tempted to distract ourselves instead of going through the process. If we constantly break the cycle that's trying to build, we remain exactly where we are. There is no movement.

I was living in New York City as I was writing this book, and having a great time. After several months, however, I took a look at my bank account and realized something needed to change and quick! My options included generating more income, which would take me away from writing, or cutting back on expenses. Keeping my goal in my sights, I decided on the latter.

I put the word out that I was looking for a place to live temporarily with low rent and minimal distractions. Within a few days, arrangements were made for me to be at a lovely retreat center in Oregon, with ample accommodations in a natural setting at a price I could afford for several months.

Everything went smoothly. Within a month, I had said goodbye to the Big Apple and hello to the Pacific Northwest. Happy ending? Not quite. Although the setting was beautiful and I was warmly received, I was miles outside of town without a car and without friends. I was seriously alone. I began hearing the echo of friends' voices who had tried to talk me out of this decision. "But you love New York," they said. "Why would you leave?" Right. Why did I leave?

Doubts started to creep in. Had I made the wrong decision? Was this a mistake? Could I get back to New York before my apartment was rented?

Sequestered and without distractions, I had to face some of the most painful loneliness I've ever know. I'd been alone before, but not like this. In the stillness, in that almost deadly silence, I heard the cries and whispers from within that I had managed to avoid for so long. With nowhere to run, it was finally time to listen and feel into the pain.

Eventually, I began to recognize the isolation as my support, my partner in finishing mybook. There was nowhere else to go, nothing else to do but write. I began to see that I had created the perfect situation to accomplish my desired outcome. I began to warm to the environment. I found a rhythm. I rested, I walked, and I wrote. It took fortitude, at first, not to bolt. But I kept referring back to how strongly I'd felt when this option first came up, and I knew I had to trust that decision and see it through.

Exercise

One of the first questions I ask a new coaching client is, "What stops you?" That way, when the going gets tough, I know what to watch for. Here's a way to hold yourself accountable when the heat is on.

Make a list of the ways in which you distract yourself when the pressure's on. Your list might include things like: watch television, talk on the phone, go shopping, play solitaire on the computer, surf the net, etc.

When the pressure is on, keep your list handy. Instead of resorting to one of your distractions, do the EDGE process on page 54 to find out what's really going on. What opportunity might you be missing if you simply distracted yourself?

Transformation is rarely career-related. You may get results there, but the fire you walk through is mostly personal. In order to experience movement, we often need to plumb the depths of our souls to discover what's hidden, what's controlling us from behind the scenes. By making an effort, we can discover what's been stopping us from fulfilling our dreams. This might not sound like a big selling point. *Plumbing the depths; standing in the fire.* But we don't get to escape the fire – ever. That's just the nature of life. We can, however, choose to participate, and this makes it easier, if not significantly more interesting.

> **In order to experience movement, we often need to plumb the depths of our souls to discover what's hidden, what's controlling us from behind the scenes.**

Being in the moment requires accepting reality - no delusions, no excuses. Often, however, what we find in the moment is pain from unfinished business. Rather than feel the pain, we distract ourselves.

It's like exercising. We're into it until we hit that edge and it starts hurting. Suddenly, the mind goes off planning your day, thinking about what your girlfriend said last night, what you'll say at the meeting this afternoon…anything to keep you from feeling the pain.

Exercise

Self discipline is an essential part of creating true change. To help you build inner strength, commit to something you'll do everyday for a month. Here are a few ideas:

Give up one thing you know isn't good for you.

Abstain from something you do that you know is a waste of time.

Meditate

Exercise

Take a walk.

Journal

Name three things you're grateful for before you go to bed.

Note: Doing something that's uncomfortable may very well cause thoughts and feelings to arise. Be aware of them, but don't react to them. Journaling helps. You may learn something very valuable about yourself.

The same goes for emotional pain. We hit a point where it hurts too much and we vacate the premises. Pain is another way of describing pressure. Life is pressing us to grow. And the only thing standing in the way is our clinging to the past. We can either stay with the process, grow, and move on, or break the container and revisit the problem at a later date. Here are three common ways we break the container of change.

Judgment

One way to go into denial and distract ourselves from reality is with judgment. Something happens in the moment, and rather than accept it for what it is, we vote on it: I like this, I don't like that.

We vote hundreds of times a day on whether or not we like what's happening, and the only thing this accomplishes is to take us out of the moment. Thoughts such as: *I don't like the noise this makes, the way she talks, the tone of his voice, the burnt pancakes,* just cause us to spin our wheels. They don't help us do anything about it. Instead, they prevent us from owning the truth which is what we can do something about. The fact is, *it does sound like that, she does talk that way, that is the tone of his voice and the pancakes are burnt.* Now, what do we *do* about it?

It's not to say that we might not prefer this sofa over that one, for example, or one person over another. In these situations you have a choice. But it's like the Serenity Prayer: "God grant me the serenity to accept the things I cannot change, the courage to change the things I can, and the wisdom to know the difference." Starting with what *is,* allows us to get to what *can be.*

Doubt

Something that saddens me is how unsupportive we can be of ourselves. Too often, we make a decision, and then when the going gets tough we doubt ourselves. Instead of staying the course, we capitulate. We question our choices. We question ourselves. We doubt our friends. We do everything but maintain a disciplined stance and push through our difficulties.

One of the greatest things we can do for ourselves is cultivate self-discipline. Inner discipline is essential, because it gives us the strength to withstand the pressure. This has very little to do with depriving yourself of something you want, and everything to do with attaining it. If you work out physically, you know how important discipline is for strengthening both your muscles and your mind. It takes a strong mind to go beyond the point where you want to stop. But if you can, the rewards are great.

What if nothing's wrong?

In addition to discipline, self love helps us overcome doubt. When things get tough, can we cut ourselves some slack like we would for others around us? Chances are, things won't go exactly according to plan. When it doesn't, can we trust that we're still okay? I have a question

I pull out when I start having doubts. *What if nothing's wrong?* We just need to improvise to get things back on track. Doubt is just another sign that we're at the edge.

Blame

Most frustration in life revolves around change. If we're frustrated, it's usually because something needs to transition and we don't know how or are afraid to make the change ourselves. In this case, we may try to put the responsibility on someone else. We get angry. We may think: *Everything would be perfect if only they would change…if only they were gone…if only they would do…*fill in the blank. Even if we're absolutely right, we're still stuck if the other person refuses to change. When we blame, we give our power to the person we're blaming. We have delivered our fate into their hands.

I once worked with a woman who was thinking of leaving her husband. She felt let down time and time again by his seeming inability to support her. She was surprised when I asked her if we could put her anger toward her husband on hold for a moment and I delicately began the process of reflecting on her. What we discovered was that she was a very difficult person to support. She expected things to be done a certain way and to her standards which were very hard to meet. In the end, she came to see a pattern of disappointment that started long before her husband. What she had built up was a very complex system protecting her from getting her hopes up and being disappointed yet again. Armed with this self-awareness, she went back to face her life.

We can sit in this kind of "log jam" for the rest of our lives, complaining and unhappy. We can stomp our feet and bang our fists and still, for some unfathomable reason, they won't change! This is probably because it's *your* life, *your* path, and *your* world that wants to expand. What's happening with them has nothing to do with you. I find this is rarely the news my clients want to hear, but it's the only thing that puts the power back into our hands and us back in control.

One of the most common ways we break the pressure is by breaking *under* the pressure. Have you ever been in a situation where everyone agrees to something, but when push comes to shove, people start pointing fingers? Instead of sticking together and accepting the outcome, they can't take the heat and start blaming someone else, saying: *It was his idea.* Maybe you've

The remedy for blame is to take responsibility for our actions, to own up to our part in the situation.

been on the side of pointing the finger, or maybe you've been the one "hung out to dry." Either way, it doesn't feel good. Some people are very supportive of new ideas until they hit a glitch. Then, they're quick with an *I told you so* attitude. Decisions often have some basis of truth. If the integrity of the container is maintained, a positive outcome can eventually be revealed even if it has to go through several revisions and it's not exactly the way everyone expected it to be.

The remedy for blame is to take responsibility for our actions, to own up to our part in the situation. Blame creates separation, and with separation there is always a lie or an illusion. In order to blame someone else, a person must turn a blind eye to their own involvement. Usually the story has to get a bit twisted to make the accusations fit. We bend the truth to protect ourselves because we cannot take the pressure, but how can we change a situation if we can't see what's really happening?

IDENTITY

Life is constantly coursing through us. We know this because when it stops...we're dead. In its coursing, Life hits a spot in us that's blocked and we feel pressure. The pressure is an indication that Life is trying to move through a space that's too small. Remember, we live in an expanding universe. One way or another, Life is going to get through. We can take comfort in knowing that Life always prevails whether it's a personal or collective block.

We welcome the pressure and become alert when we feel it. It means that Life is pressing for change. The question is, who are we in the midst of this pressure? Are we that which is being changed or the Life that is creating the change?

If we are identified with that which is passing away, we may have a difficult time of it. Am I my job title? My wealth? My physical property? Someone's wife? Mother? Husband? Son? Everything manmade in the physical world will eventually pass away. Granted some things we've made will unfortunately take generations to decompose. But I am speaking more of manmade institutions like banking, religion, government, corporations, education and even marriage. We are already seeing a breakdown because these institutions are merely a substitute - money as a substitute for love, education for wisdom, commerce for caring for one another.

We are not our clothes, our cars, our bank accounts, our houses. Spiritual teachers for thousands of years have cautioned about becoming attached to material objects. All it takes is one natural event like a tsunami or a hurricane to wipe away all of those material objects. All that remains are the people themselves. They all say the same thing afterward. "I'm just glad we're alive."

Spiritual teachings might say that we are not even our bodies, our thoughts or our emotions. We may think and feel things, but we are not those thoughts or feelings. Our senses are simply there as a means of experiencing life.

Who are we then? What is our true identity? Personally, I find this most easily understood by an expression attributed to the teacher, Jesus: *Be in the world but not of it.* For me, these words point to the idea that our presence in this world is of a dual nature. We are both human and being, both physical and spiritual at the same time. We are both the observer and the participant, engaged but not attached.

There is more to my story about exercising and discovering edge. At the point of feeling the discomfort, it occurred to me to shift my identity from the part of me that was hurting to the Life moving *through* my body. As I allowed my awareness to shift over to the flow of energy, the flow of Life within, I was amazed when all of a sudden I was able to stretch far beyond where I had gone before.

We spoke earlier about looking through your eyes and asking yourself who's looking. We called that the *observer.* Once again, look through your eyes and become aware of the part of yourself that is observing. Now, look at someone else and ask: *Who's looking through their eyes? Is it possible it's the same presence?* Might we call that presence Life? If so, we could say that what we are seeing is Life looking for itself.

Now think about Life moving through every living thing, longing to re-unite with itself. Imagine that feeling that comes over you when taking in the splendor of nature – a pristine mountain range or a perfect rose. Could it be that the awe we feel is actually the sensation of Life finding itself?

Life stirs us from within to bring forth new creation. At the same time, it calls to us from the world with the pieces from which to construct that creation. Our longings must navigate their way through a land mine of old feelings and memories to surface in our consciousness. Meanwhile, our callings must overcome the distractions of day-to-day life. We stand at a crossover point and receive them both. What we create from that point has meaning because it comes from our true identity.

When the pressure is on, it's helpful to remember who we really are. We are not the changing circumstances, nor our titles, nor our things. We are both the inspiration from within and the artist using all of these elements as our medium to create a masterpiece called *our lives.*

Exercise

Make a list of all the roles you play in your life: mother, daughter, sister, wife, father, son, brother, husband, lover, boss, worker, leader, friend, coach, volunteer, caregiver, churchgoer, (job title), etc. Who are you without your titles? Write about it.

Think of all of the adjectives used to describe yourself: happy, fun, cynical, playful, mysterious, adventurous, fearful, cautious, generous, optimistic, pessimistic, careful, careless, reckless, innovative, short-sighted, etc. These words create energetic "forms". Who are you after the "forms" are taken away? Write.

Knowing this will help you stay focused when change starts happening and outmoded parts of yourself start falling away.

TRUE DESIRE

There is a major difference in the outcome between choices made from true passion and choices made by default. The first leads to growth and happiness while the second simply replicates the past.

If we want true change, we must learn to differentiate between the two. One is tried by fire, while the second is often a reaction. One leaves room for Life to work its magic, while the other resists Life. We make room for Life by showing up in the moment, even if its difficult and then staying until a decision is obvious.

You can bang two pieces of wood together all day long and you are not going to start a fire. In order to transform a situation, we must turn up the heat. "Take the high road," as they say. Raise the frequency. We turn up the heat by coming from a place of love. In this way, we align with something above separation. *PROXIMITY* then keeps the fire burning until our thoughts and feelings run clear.

One night, I was having trouble falling asleep. My mind was going everywhere. Instead of distracting myself, I decided to face the demons and find out what was really going on in there. I finally realized I was lonely, a fact I'd been avoiding since I'd gotten divorced. I realized I would do just about anything to avoid feeling that pain, but now it was time to face it.

I opened a dialogue with myself. "What do I want?" I considered. "What am I missing?" *I want someone to be with.* There it was - the words I had been avoiding because I felt there was nothing I could do about it. But this time, instead of denying it, I let myself imagine what it would be like to cuddle up with his arms around me. I let myself take in that feeling. Safe, secure, held, loved. The physical sense of his body next to mine. Strong, intimate.

As I defined what I longed for, the outline of what I wanted emerged. I saw how avoiding the loneliness cheated me of the chance to get in touch with my true desires. Pretending I was fine, I missed the opportunity to dream. Without acknowledging what we want, how can we ever attract it? This is yet another example of our mirror reality. By resisting, we create the opposite of what we want.

Ignoring the fact that I miss being with a partner, the heat never gets turned up around relationship and there are only more cold and lonely nights. Denying access to these thoughts and feelings, I never give myself the chance to work through what might be stopping me from having that kind of love in my life. And surprisingly, by allowing myself to dream about what would make me happy, I ended up feeling happy. Taking it one step further, I created a *wish list* – basically a large sheet of paper I taped to the wall. Every time I saw a couple together and felt a twinge of envy, instead of running from the feeling I added it to my wish list. *I want to stroll through the park hand in hand. I want to steal a quick kiss. I want a romantic dinner.* Getting in touch with our desires allows us to draw them closer.

For so long now, we have resisted love, often leaving us afraid and sad, disconnected and alone. What would it take for that cycle of pain and suffering to be broken, for the illusion of separation to be shattered? What could change? What would emerge from such freedom and joy? There is only one way to find out, and that is by going all the way through, past the edge – to have the passion and commitment to be absolute about it – to let something be known on earth, to change absolutely. The purpose of *PROXIMITY* is to allow the truth to be revealed.

Exercise

Think of something you long for – a relationship, more money, a different career. When feelings of sadness or frustration arise because you don't have it yet, start a wish list. Instead of thinking, "Why don't I have this?" write on your wish list: I want _____,

Your wish list can be a sheet of paper you dedicate to holding your dreams. I used a large piece of drawing paper and wrote my desires in colored markers. If you see a picture of what you want in a magazine, cut it out and put it on your wish list. The idea is to stop denying what we want and start admitting it. When we do, we can start to attract it.

Courage

Commit to coming from a place of LOVE

Find your right PROXIMITY and wait for clarity

When the path is clear, have the COURAGE to act.

Catching the Updraft

*W*e begin by committing ourselves to coming from a place of *LOVE*. In other words, we declare that we are committed to being oriented in something that's true. Then, like a motorcycle rider, we take to the road and for awhile it's smooth sailing. Eventually, there comes a turn in the road, and it's time to amp up our attention. Enter *PROXIMITY*. Proximity is our relationship to the world around us. Like the cyclist, we may need to adjust our speed by slowing down or accelerating, whatever is required to keep our balance and remain upright on the road. But none of this is possible without the willingness to go with what the road brings and to accept what *is*. This is the time for *COURAGE*.

There's no glory unless we risk suspending the known for the unknown and leap blindly into the mystery.

The more proficient we become, the smoother the ride. We can maintain our balance by adjusting our proximity as we go. Sometimes change requires the willingness to risk imbalance in order to get to the next point of balance. If you think about it, most extreme sports involve this combination of balance, imbalance, and re-balance. Skateboarders lift off, hoping to find balance upon landing. Surfers relinquish the comfort of floating in order to rise and experience the thrill of the wave. Pole vaulters sail. Horseback riders jump. Football players go long. Baseball players swing. Basketball players shoot. There's no glory unless we risk suspending the known for the unknown and leap blindly into the mystery. It's the very fact that we don't know what will happen once we release the ball, the pole, or the swing that makes it exhilarating.

We live for those moments of freedom – nights out, weekends off, tropical vacations - as if they're rare when, in fact, freedom is our birthright. We play it safe in our attempt to protect ourselves from dying, and instead we die of boredom.

As soon as we start to feel movement, we clutch. Instead of thrilling in the excitement, we look around for something to grab onto. This immediately breaks the flow, leaving us to work our way back, at which point we will probably stop ourselves again and have to start over. It's a futile cycle, and one we would do well to break.

Like everything else in our world of opposites, we stop when we should go. We work so hard to create opportunities, and then when they show up we hesitate.

A friend of mine, Adam, was working at a job he wasn't crazy about, with people who often acted crazy. He'd been at his job a long time and it was no longer challenging. He longed for something more interesting. He was offered a great job at another company that was very creative for substantially more money. Surprisingly, he found himself hesitating. It wasn't that he liked the work he did at his current job. In fact, he'd been miserable for quite awhile, and most of the people he enjoyed working with had already left. What was there to hold onto? We laughed. Was it the company softball team? The cafeteria? Clearly, it wasn't about what he was leaving behind, although he did have some attachments there. More likely it was the fear of the unknown. When Adam looked at the new opportunity, all he could see was a skeleton of possibility, a rough sketch of what it might be like. Would he be good at the new job? Would he meet their expectations? Would he succeed or fail? He had no way of knowing until he tried.

COURAGE is about taking action. In this regard, a question that often comes up is: How do I know what the right thing is? We may feel attracted to someone, but wonder if they're right for us. We may want to get away from a situation, but wonder if this is really the right time. This is the purpose of coming from a place of love and letting all of our fear-based thoughts and feelings burn away. The point of *PROXIMITY* is to hold steady and wait until our direction becomes so clear that there is no question.

When you know, you know in a moment. All becomes clear. You feel as if your whole body has aligned in a forward direction and is ready to move. It's a big cosmic YES. The next step and the next are laid out before you in a natural progression. There might be practical details to work out, such as travel plans, résumés, and meetings, but the doors will open easily.

Until then, holding steady can be difficult. The pressure builds and we want to do something. Anything! Acting prematurely will yield results, but it's usually more of what we've already got, not the quantum change we seek. A great question to ask at this point is: Where's the joy? Which path leads to expansion and greater happiness? This re-aligns us with love and the present moment.

Exercise

Think of a time in your life when you acted with courage. Write about it.

Did you know you were going to do what you did?

How did you arrive at the decision?

Were you afraid?

 Did you have help?

What was the risk?

How did you decide to take the risk?

What did it feel like while you were in the updraft?

What did it feel like after?

What can you take away from this experience that might help you next time you need to be courageous?

POWERED BY LIFE

In the physics of fire, the molecules released from the wood are lighter than air and so they rise. This rising creates a natural movement called updraft. We also need movement when we're making changes in our lives. That action can either be self-propelled or in the flow. We can either use our own fuel or be powered by Life.

Moving under our own steam usually means that we have to be really motivated because given the option, most of us would rather be comfortable. Maybe I should speak for myself. I'd rather be comfortable.

Too often, the most common motivation for change is pain or anger.

Fortunately, Life doesn't allow us to stay comfortable for too long. First, opportunity knocks at our door with a little inspiration. If we pretend we're not listening, it usually knocks a little harder. Still not listening? Down comes the door. Finally, still not willing to leave the comfort of home? Oops. House-afire. Oh, wait. Fire. Perfect! That's exactly what we needed in the first place to get things moving.

Too often, the most common motivation for change is pain or anger. When I left my corporate job to move to the wine country of Northern California, people said things like: "Wow, it takes so much courage to change everything." The truth is, I was so unhappy that moving was much easier than staying. It wasn't courage that motivated me. It was pain.

Sometimes, we use anger to motivate us: *I'm mad as hell and I'm not gonna take it anymore.* In a fury, we quit or leave or burn a bridge we cannot return across. This kind of change might get us where we want to go eventually, but usually we end up jumping into a situation similar to or worse than the one we were in. It's the old adage: *Out of the frying pan and into the fire.* We see this in choices about relationships. People escape from one relationship and then, because they don't want to be alone, they jump right into another one that's the same or worse because nothing's really changed inside of them.

Unless we take the time to understand our present situation, we are likely bound for more of the same. We've talked about the light that's produced from fire. This means gaining understanding, awareness, and growth. We could say that unless we *grow* from our experiences, we're destined to repeat ourselves until we do.

EMBRACING MOVEMENT

We talked earlier about re-sensitizing to our feelings in order to recognize when we've hit an edge. We also need to pay attention to fear in relationship to the updraft, specifically the fear of movement. Do you know the feeling you get when you're strapped into a rollercoaster and it starts to move? Maybe there's a little jolt, a false start, and then it gets going. You know the feeling that comes up in you? Uh oh!

We get this same feeling when we start to move into the updraft. We've been at a dead stop in our lives, and then suddenly we start to feel motion. We get scared because we equate movement with fear, angst, or dread. Instead of going with it, we resist. Frightened by the feeling of motion, we apply the brakes, latching onto whatever's closest at hand. It's worth noting what we grab onto, because it's usually our standard excuses: *I don't have the money. I don't have time. I've got the kids.* This is when we manifest the car breaking down and eating up all the money we had for our new adventure. This is when the kids get sick and we can't go. This is when you don't do it – whatever *it* is – because your husband or wife thinks it's a stupid idea. We feel the movement, become afraid, and look around for some way to stall the process. Of course, we always find it!

As we become familiar with the stages of true change, we are soon able to identify them when they arise: *Oh, here's the part where things start to heat up. Right. Here's the part where the old thoughts and feelings come up. Fear? Great. Here's the movement I've been waiting for.* By recognizing the stages, we can let go into them instead of resisting. You paid your money to take the ride, so go with it! Let out a big *yahoo* and let 'er rip! You may scream the whole time, but let it be a scream of excitement because you're willingly, even passionately participating. It's like shooting the rapids. Once the raft leaves the shore, there's no turning back. But you're in for the ride of your life. You can either fight it or get into it, but going upstream is not an option.

When we allow for understanding to come, we eventually find ourselves caught up in the moment. Then we are in the flow. When clarity comes, we have the energy we need for movement. Can you remember a time when you got to a point of clarity and you knew exactly what you needed to do? You probably felt a surge of energy that gave you the power you needed to make the move.

We are like lovers running toward one another across a sunlit meadow, caught in a magnetism that will not be denied.

Most importantly, true change is fueled by attraction rather than desperation or anger. We are literally carried in the arms of Life because we have *chosen* to honor the longing in our hearts and to move toward that which calls to us from the world. We know that we are on the right track because of an increased sense of lightness and energy. We are like lovers running toward one another across a sunlit meadow, caught in a magnetism that will not be denied.

There are three things I have learned in studying change that keep us from taking action. They are *risk, payoff* and *attachments*. All change involves risking *something*. There is always a payoff for keeping *something* the same. We hold onto the status quo because we're attached to *something*. Find out what those *something's* are, and we're freed up to take the next step.

Risk

We stand upon a precipice, the edge of the chasm. The bridge is built, and all we have to do is walk across it. Guaranteed, there is one thing that will occur if we do: things will change. Take that step and your life will never be the same again. *You* will never be the same. The predictable will become unpredictable. This idea most likely carries both excitement and fear, thrill and horror. We want something new, even as we fear the unknown. We want to break up our old routine, but we also want to know what happens next.

> ### There is always some element of risk when we step into the unknown. The truth is, life is much riskier outside the flow than in it.

This brings us to risk. There is always some element of risk when we step into the unknown. The truth is, life is much riskier *outside* the flow than in it. We move with the design of Life when we are in the flow. Outside of it, we reside in chaos. Somehow, we have come to believe that we can prevent our worst fears from happening by avoiding them. Hummm…. As we say in Shadow Work, "How's that working for you?" The answer is undoubtedly, "Not very well."

My friend, Adam, was afraid to change jobs. On the surface, there was no logical explanation of why he wouldn't want the new, better job. But under the surface, he realized he was afraid of failing. He worried about going to his new job and not being able to measure up.

When I asked him how "not measuring up" made him feel, he said, "Hopeless." I then asked him how he felt in his current job. Eyes widening, he replied, "Hopeless." Adam began to see that allowing his fear to dictate, he was guaranteed failure and hopelessness. He already had it. But trying something new at least gave him a fighting chance for success and happiness.

We bring upon ourselves that which we fear. The very thing we spend our whole lives avoiding is the very thing we end up creating time and time again. Life just keeps hammering away until we finally take the risk, leap into the abyss, and fail or succeed.

We are more likely to accept risk if we can identify it. Ask yourself: *What's the risk for me if I....?* Your answer might be to take a chance on love, or forgive your father, or accept your shortcomings. It could be anything. By asking yourself this question and considering the answer, you will most likely realize that you have already been creating the very thing you've been afraid would happen. *A woman is afraid of leaving a loveless relationship because she's afraid she'll never find love again.* Fail to take the risk and she is assured of a loveless relationship.

A man is afraid of going after his dream because he's afraid of failure. If he never goes after his dream, failure is guaranteed. Give it a try and, who knows? He may just succeed.

You have nothing to lose by trying something new. In fact, you are more likely to get what you want by changing your game than sticking to the old one. Risk masks itself as fear when it remains concealed.

Identifying Risk

Exercise

Knowing the risk makes it much easier to take it. This is a great process to use when you're afraid to make a change.

PART 1: Start by identifying what you want to change. Write it down. What's the risk for you to do that? In other words, what might happen? Sometimes the first answer you get is the one. Sometimes you have to go deeper. Try asking yourself what the risk is if the first thing happens. Example: What's the risk to start dating again? I'm afraid I can't trust my judgment. What's the risk if it turns out you misjudge someone? I'll have gotten my hopes up and been disappointed again. What's the risk of being disappointed again? I'll end up alone. So the risk is, you might end up alone. Get the idea? Dig deep.

PART 2: The thing about risks is that they may or may not happen. What we fear, we most surely bring upon ourselves. After identifying your risk, look to see how you might already be creating that in your life. Example: So, the risk is that you might end up alone? Yes. What is your life like now? I'm alone. So, without taking the risk you're already alone. Taking the risk, you may end up alone but you might not. How do you feel about taking the risk now? I've got nothing to lose. I think I'll take it.

That said, sometimes we're just not ready to take the risk and that's okay, too. At least you know what it is. Then, if you choose, you can take steps that might build your confidence and move you toward taking the risk, like going into therapy, going back to school, getting help from a friend. In the end, if your answer is no, honor yourself for having the courage to take care of yourself.

Payoff

Payoff is another component that is helpful to understand when meeting with resistance to change. The definition of *payoff* has to do with a hidden benefit of negative behavior. In this case it's some negative benefit you get for staying with a negative situation. *What is the payoff for staying with your current situation?*

In most cases, *negative payoff* has something to do with playing it safe and keeping ourselves small. That way, we never have to find out if we're good enough, smart enough, talented enough, or brave enough.

I once worked with two sisters, Martha and Rosa, who had a very dominant mother. Though both women were adults, they remained locked in a mother-daughter relationship more suited to children.

Life in their family revolved around the mother and her needs. If she needed something, the girls would drop what they were doing and go over to help. For Martha, with two small children of her own, this was never easy. She also had to deal with flack from her husband about running out. Rosa, who was single, was seemingly more available and found herself staying home with mom instead of having a social life of her own. The two women were drawn by a sense of duty, but there was also an upside. As long as mom was making all of the decisions, the "girls" got to remain under their mother's protective umbrella. Neither woman had to take responsibility for her own choices. This was a case of *mother knows best* where the children had not been raised to grow up and think for themselves.

By the end of our first session, the women began to realize that they were not betraying anyone by putting their own lives and families first. They also realized that letting their mother make the decisions had, in some ways, been easier. If something went wrong, she would take care of it. This was the negative payoff.

In order to take their lives back, they saw that they would have to make decisions for themselves and risk making mistakes. In the end, this was a much better example for Martha to set for her children. Martha and Rosa agreed that they would support each others' independence and encourage their mother to stand on her own as well, though, this was no longer their responsibility.

A negative payoff masks our inaction. It takes brutal honesty to expose the payoff and take responsibility for our actions. Anytime you blame someone else, you can pretty well guess there's a negative payoff in there somewhere. If it's his or her fault, you won't have to take responsibility for your actions.

When we blame someone else for our inability to change, we've also just handed them our power. In order to reclaim it, we need to search for the source of our fear and find out what we haven't wanted to know about ourselves. The moment we own up to our fear, we reclaim our power – the power that drives change.

Exercise

This process helps you understand the negative benefit you get from keeping things the same.

Describe a situation you've been wanting to change. Now consider these questions:

What is the negative benefit for staying with your current situation?

How does keeping things the same keep you safe, let you play small?

What does staying the same keep you from ever having to find out about yourself?

Who have you turned your power over to?

What would you have to do to reclaim your power? (Hint: This has nothing to do with the other person doing anything.)

If you keep going the way you've been going, what's most likely to happen?

How might things be different if you allow them to change?

Attachment

Living in the material world can be tricky. As I said earlier, there's this matter of being in the world while being detached. Living in the paradox is a very Zen thing. You can't really live in the world without being connected, but you have to be in the world without being attached.

I found while living in the spiritual community that, as long as I didn't get attached to outcomes, I was able to keep my heart open. This, of course, is how we stay in the moment where life happens and change occurs. The minute I was more focused on getting results than the quality of the process, I saw how quickly relationships began to unravel. When I stayed in the moment, trusting the process would work out one way or another – and maybe not how I expected it to – meetings became inspired and meaningful.

This kind of detachment may seem like a lot to ask when rent money may be on the line but, ultimately, Life has its way anyway. Remember the life moving through us, coordinating us? That is always in play if only we release our grip and let it move us. I have a favorite saying when I feel myself holding on too tightly: I only have to know *what* I want. The *how* is up to Life. In other words, I don't need to know all of the details. I am a great one for making plans – business plans, life plans. Recently, feeling anxious about how things were going, I made a ten year plan. Then I tried to detail how all of this was going to happen. The more details, the more unsettled I felt. Finally, I reminded myself, *I don't need to know how, just what.* I scrapped the plan and replaced it with a very simple 6-point vision of what I wanted:

1) a home that's a sanctuary

2) a relationship with a generous, loving man

3) a secure financial future

4) a creatively stimulating community

5) fun and supportive friends

6) a healthy, happy family

As soon as I did that, things began to rearrange. The home in the country I thought was so far off in my future became a more immediate possibility. I returned to a pottery class, and then remembered what a wonderful sense of community I'd felt there. I felt my heart open to receiving more love. If we can let go of our attachment to outcome, we free ourselves up to be available to Life.

In addition to attachment to outcome, we may also be attached to material possessions – our four bedroom house, our BMW, our designer clothing. They become a part of who we are just like our roles as wife, father, parent, caregiver, poor, rich, and so on. As we talked about in the section on *PROXIMITY*, these things can disappear all too easily and, with them, our centering if our identity is tied to them. Can we be *present* regardless of our external circumstances? In order for true change to occur, change beyond our own ideas, we must learn how to detach ourselves. We do this by letting go of our *worldly* identity and staying in our true identity as an instrument through which Life plays.

Change involves the unpredictable, which can make us uncomfortable. Anything can happen! Rather than embracing the adventure, we tend to prefer the status quo. As the saying goes, "Better the devil you know than the devil you don't."

Ultimately, letting go involves trust. Can we trust that if we let go, something better will take its place? Too often, we keep mediocre relationships and situations alive because we think we need them to get our needs met. *If I let go of this awful job, I may not get another one. What if I walk away from this relationship and nothing better comes along?* In other words, what if this is as good as it gets? We won't know unless we try. And we're guaranteed a life of dissatisfaction and emptiness if we stay.

Ultimately, letting go involves trust. Can we trust that if we let go, something better will take its place?

Have you ever seen one of those movies where a person is dangling off the edge of a cliff and in order to save themselves, they have to let go of what they're holding and reach for someone's outstretched arm? This is literally a cliff hanger moment! They either take a chance or fall to their death.

Such is the case with change. Inevitably, there comes a moment when we must let go of the familiar and reach for something new. Of all the blocks that can stop us from changing, one of

Exercise

Think of something you want to change.

What are your expectations around the outcome? Do you have a set idea of how things should turn out? See if you can broaden your definition of the change, leaving room for Life to play a part.

Make a list of everything you might lose if things change. Now make a list of everything you might gain. How do they compare? How attached are you to what you might lose? Can you trust that if you let go, something better will take its place?

the main reasons is attachments. We become attached to the known. Even if it's painful, it's still familiar, and we hang onto it because we feel safer living with the known than the unknown.

FINDING YOUR COMFORT LEVEL WITH CHANGE

It's helpful to know what type of person you are when it comes to change. Are you a risk taker? Conservative? Cautious? Just how comfortable are you with leaping into the unknown?

Personally, I am quite at ease with leaping first and then looking around for a place to land although the older I get, the less inclined I am to do it without knowing there's some sort of a soft landing. A former boyfriend preferred to have a plan for everything. You can imagine the dynamics that went on between us. I was always wondering why things were taking so long, and he was frustrated with the chaos.

Much to my dismay, after we broke up, I found myself having similar arguments with myself. This was more than a bit distressing. I thought I'd rid myself of that problem! Instead, there was still that fiery part of me that wanted to be compulsive, make changes, and live what I thought was an exciting life! From out of the shadows, however, appeared my heretofore unknown inner conservative, who wanted everything recorded and accounted for. I tried ignoring her but she started keeping me up at night with worrying, planning, and plotting. Needless to say, I found it more than a bit harrowing one day when there was such internal turmoil that I wanted to break up with *myself*. Realizing the insanity of it all, I decided I'd better start exploring balance.

One of the teachings I learned in my spiritual training is that *Life always moves from the known to the unknown.* We must always start from where we are to move to where we want to be. We never completely move from something we know to something we know nothing about without some connecting link in between. The ancient symbol of the mandorla - two interlocking circles - helps us visualize this concept:

The Mandorla

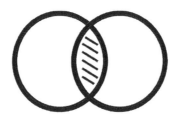

Known   Overlap   Unknown

Anytime you hear yourself saying your choices are "either/or", it's time for the mandorla. Beth, a young client of mine, came to me confused about whether or not she should leave her husband. When they first got together, she felt strong and in control. Over time, she felt like he wasn't respecting her. She knew something needed to change but she wasn't sure if she was ready for something final.

I drew the two interlocking circles. On one side I wrote the word go and on the other I wrote stay. "Now what's in between?" I asked.

She thought about it for a moment. Then a smile came to her face and she replied, "I could stay and draw better boundaries or I could leave and still maintain a connection." Either of those choices allowed Beth to get to a better place than where she was without making a final break.

Looking back, I realize that the mandorla might have provided a suitable compromise for my conservative partner and me - him being willing to make changes as long as we had a plan, and me being okay with waiting as long as I knew change was coming. I never got the chance to find out if that would have worked, but I have come to terms with the two parts of myself. I had to release my polarized identity as both a daring person and a cautious person in order to find a comfortable balance between the two. My ability to plan and budget now gives foundation to my risk taking.

As simple as it is, the mandorla is an amazing tool. It shows us the bridge that gets us from where we are to where we want to be. It helps us find balance so we don't have to feel unsafe when making changes. And it can point us to our next step when it seems like we have none or we don't like either that we can see.

Exercise

The mandorla is a powerful tool to use when you feel like you only have two options and you don't like either one. It's also a great way to find steps to your ultimate goal.

Describe the situation with which you're working. Name the two choices. How could you create a hybrid option from those two choices?

EXAMPLE: Steven has been having problems at work. First he was promised a promotion he wasn't given. Then he was promised work in which he could earn commissions. But his boss keeps him busy with administrative work and he has little time for sales. He can't decide if he should fight for better pay or just quit. The two options Steven's considering are fight or quit.

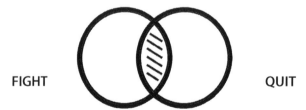

A third option would be to define his bottom line for himself, then communicate that at work. This contains elements of both options. He's speaking up for himself but he's also prepared to quit if his needs aren't met.

LEARNING TO FLY

The ultimate purpose of going back and forth between *LOVE* and *PROXIMITY* is to generate enough heat to create an updraft. We focus on what we want, blocks come up, we observe and transform them, re-align with our desires and do it all over again until the way is clear.

Eventually, what we want seems easier and more attainable, while what has stopped us loses its hold. *Her mom can no longer push her buttons. He can listen to his wife without thinking she's trying to control him. She can let go of that co-dependent relationship. He can take a chance on himself by starting his own business.*

This is the updraft, the current, the flow, the cosmic YES. If we let go into it, we fly. When that happens, we may feel a bit disoriented because we're not used to it. After all, how many of us have learned to fly? We need to re-orient.

This is the updraft, the current, the flow, the cosmic YES. If we let go into it, we fly.

To help on this account, I have included some spiritual flying lessons. These will hopefully help you feel more secure once you find yourself taking flight.

Lesson 1: You're Flying in Something

While snorkeling in Hawaii, I floated with schools of fish as they gracefully shifted from one direction to the next. I thought, "This is the closest I'll ever come to flying." It was an amazing feeling, weightless and free.

There is a lot to learn about flying from both fish and birds. Their common experience is that they are *in* something when they're moving - fish in water and birds in the air. Picture a bird flying and you see their wings pushing against the air. Likewise, fish use their bodies to push against the water. When we're flying there is also something that keeps us afloat. It's our own personal atmosphere. When we're in a positive and loving place, our atmosphere is refined and light. It's full and rich. It raises us up. When we give in to blame, anger and shame, our atmosphere begins to disintegrate. How can we fly without the substance to fly within?

Sometimes we talk about this substance as a person's energy. Some people just feel good to be around while others feel really awful. It's said that animals have the ability to read this kind of energy. They know instinctively who to trust. Personally, I've had the experience of gaining amazing insights and even healing just being in the presence of someone's atmosphere.

The clearer our energy field, the better reception we get from our inner voice. Our inner knowing comes in loud and clear, helping us to navigate our way. This is another reason why we commit to coming from a place of love. From that place, it's easier to tap into our intuition, also known as our gut. I don't know how many times I've heard the story of a man meeting a woman for the first time and telling his friend, "I'm going to marry her." And then doing so! It happened to my brother. The heart opens, and the message is clear.

As you gain altitude, the air thins and you may experience a change in atmosphere. To acclimate, try some of the more refined attitudes such as thankfulness, respectfulness and compassion while avoiding some of the courser activities like blame, gossip and judgment.

Lesson 2: You Asked for It

I used to have trouble flying on airplanes. Finally, one day as we were lifting off, I told myself: You asked for this flight. You booked it. You've asked the pilot to fly you to where you're going. You've gotten on in one place and will get off in another. You have chosen all of this. This is your choice.

Realizing that I had asked to take the flight and I was not a victim helped calm me. It was my choice. I wanted it – and I was getting it. When we remember that we are simply getting what we've asked for, our angst is replaced with a sense of adventure. We can choose to tell ourselves: Right. I wanted to go somewhere I've never been before and now I'm doing it. Although there may still be some concern about the unknown, at least you know you're on a course you've set.

Lesson 3: Attitude Gives you Altitude

There is a great opportunity to enjoy the ride when we're rising. During this fragile time of early flight, however, we can be pulled down if we allow ourselves to be caught up in limiting thoughts and feelings. Uplifting thoughts such as blessing, gratitude, and forgiveness keep us afloat and move us forward in this sea of substance.

If we go to bed every night grateful for what we've received and get up every morning thankful for what is yet to come, the flight becomes effortless. The fear is dispelled and the turbulence calmed.

Even though you may not totally believe it, keep a positive attitude. Here are some helpful phrases:

Bless this day.

I'm grateful for what this day has brought.

I chose this.

I'm getting what I asked for.

Thank you.

Lesson 4: Jet Lag

When we make radical shifts, we are, in a sense, moving into a new time zone. You may experience drowsiness. Take time to rest.

IT'S ABOUT THE JOURNEY

Once in the air, we're present and in the zone, in the moment, and in the flow. We have surrendered and become adventurers exploring the mystery.

On this grand adventure, we encounter other explorers who have also let go. We begin to move in synch with one another like fish in the sea of Life. Miraculously, out of chaos comes order, and it is an order beyond our own making. This order is timeless and sustainable for as long as it needs to be. Then it shifts and moves again. We turn and change with the current, holding onto nothing longer than what is relevant. Free of roles, our identity is flexible and fluid.

Miraculously, out of chaos comes order, and it is an order beyond our own making.

Like riding that motorcycle, we adjust our speed to what we and the bike can handle, sometimes slowing, sometimes accelerating. Overcoming the urge to resist the turns, we courageously lean into them, becoming one with the bike, the road, and everything around us. We're focused and on the edge, heart racing, all for that bit of freedom that feels like flying.

This is our dance with *LOVE*, *PROXIMITY*, and *COURAGE*. Love is the passion that draws us. Proximity is what brings clarity, but nothing changes without the courage to ignore fear and throw ourselves into the adventure without reservation. Otherwise, we reside forever in the mundane. Without letting go and taking a chance, we are doomed to safety, predictability, and boredom.

Getting back to my friend, Adam, he made the change to his new job but that's not the end of the story. Within six months, the company ran into financial difficulties and he was laid off. You might be thinking that Adam's process of *LOVE, PROXIMITY* and *COURAGE* didn't work. Quite the contrary. With the self-confidence Adam gained from taking this new job, and the severance pay he received when he was laid off, he started his own business.

And Beth? She went back to her husband and told him what she was and wasn't willing to accept. Much to her surprise, he had missed the feisty woman he had married and was happy to see her showing up with more attitude. The spark is back in their marriage.

With both of these people, something unexpected happened. They took a leap into the unknown and were met by Life showing up on the other side. We can choose to live memorable lives on the edge of our seats, or coast along. Is it possible that it's the monotony of life that does us in? How about dreams unfulfilled? Do we take a chance and live the life we know deep inside is available, or do we betray ourselves day after day because we just won't let go?

I once got invited to go up in a small plane to watch a group of skydivers jump. Reaching altitude, they told me to scoot back as they removed the door. One at a time, these courageous young men stepped out onto the wing and then…let go, just…let go. Without that moment of risk and release, it's just another plane ride.

These are our lives. Are we willing to set them on fire? To render them unrecognizable? To turn the old to ashes and activate the seeds of the new? When the way becomes clear, do we have the courage to take it?

Tools

Commit to coming from a place of LOVE

Find your right PROXIMITY and wait for clarity

When the path is clear, have the COURAGE to act.

Introduction

This section provides tools to help you facilitate change in your life.

WORKING THE PROCESS

Steve's story provides an example of how to apply *LOVE*, *PROXIMITY*, and *COURAGE* to one's life.

THE PATH OF PAIN

This emotional map describes the order in which we move away from Love, and the journey we must take to return to Love.

THE COMPASS OF LOVE

The Compass of Love is an invaluable navigational tool for change. So often in the process of change, thoughts and feelings arise. Old patterns we've been entrenched in, keep us locked in place. The Compass of Love helps you understand the real meaning behind your feelings. They can then guide you back to Love and to the moment. The Compass of Love also assists you to understand your thoughts and to re-wire them back to truth.

Working the Process

We've talked about what it means to commit to love, find your right proximity, and have the courage to act. Here's an example of how to use them together.

Steve is twenty-five years old, lives with his parents and works at a phone store. It's not a bad job, but it doesn't pay much, he has trouble with his boss, and, more importantly, he'd rather be doing something else. Unfortunately, he doesn't know what that is. Here's how Steve can use *LOVE, PROXIMITY* and *COURAGE* to change his life.

Commit to Love

Steve's first step is to promise himself that he will do something with his life that he feels passionate about, something that will hold his interest, and be fulfilling. At this stage, no action is required, only the promise. I will do something I care about with my life. Steve writes this on a piece of paper and puts it on his mirror so he is reminded of his pledge on a daily basis. He has now found due north and his course is set.

The next step is to observe what happens. What comes up once he's made his declaration? For example, he may notice a negativity his father has about his own job. Maybe he hears his mother showing a lack of confidence in his father's ability to be successful. Steve may notice that he doesn't have an adequate role model to guide him. All of this is valuable information. He may want to write some of it down or talk with a friend to help him connect with the information.

This is a good time for the **Compass of Love.** By exploring the love, sadness, fear and anger in Steve's life, he can get to the root of some of the "baggage" he's carrying that gets in the way of living the life he dreams of living.

Find Your Right Proximity

Now it's time for *PROXIMITY*. Steve's challenge is to take the emphasis off his job and put it on finding his passion. Doing this automatically changes the proximity to his work. If he knows that this job is not everything to him, but a means to an end, it takes the pressure off. Once he changes that perspective, odds are he will begin to enjoy his day more.

Until now, Steve hasn't changed anything on the outside, only on the inside. He's made a commitment to himself to find his passion. He's now watching what comes up mentally and emotionally in his current situation. He takes the emphasis off his current job, releasing any attachment to that. This is the equivalent of pulling up anchor so he can begin to move.

Back to Love

Now we come back to Steve's passion. What is it? He may or may not know. If he does, he can begin to explore possibilities. This is a good time to consider his hopes and dreams. What kind of life does he see for himself? He may have a lot of ideas or he might not have any. If Steve doesn't know what will make his heart sing right now, it may be because other things have covered it up and they will be uncovered in his process of alternating LOVE and PROXIMITY. In the meantime, he can look for clues by noticing what attracts him or what someone else has that attracts him. This is a good time for him to create a **Wish List**.

Back to Proximity

As Steve gets clearer about what he wants, doubts may surface. Instead of seeing possibilities, he sees all of the reasons why it can't happen. Not enough money, not enough time, not the right connections, and so on.

It's time to keep the heat on, hold steady and wait for signs of change. In the meantime, it's important for Steve to avoid dissipating the pressure. Keeping his **List of Distractions** handy will help. He can also watch for **judgments**, **doubts** and **blame** that might blur the truth and keep him spinning his wheels.

Flying Lesson # 2 is a good reminder to Steve that whatever happens – he asked for it by initiating change. Everything that happens does so to move him toward his greatest joy. The best response for whatever comes during this time is *thank you*. Whether Steve gets fired, gets a raise, gets laid off or quits, it is all evidence that something is on the move and he's in the arms of transformative change. This is also a good time for the question: ***What if nothing's wrong?***

Courage

Steve will draw on courage throughout the process – to hold steady, change proximity, and maybe even to admit to himself what he really wants. When his true path becomes clear, it's time for the courage to act. Steve's path may require going back to school or getting some technical training. It might involve moving, apprenticing or working in partnership with someone. To find the courage, he can assess the risks of change, identify the negative payoffs for keeping things the same, and see what attachments he's holding onto.

On his new path, he continues to check his course by asking the question, ***Where's the joy?*** If it's missing, he adjusts his proximity to gain a clearer perspective. With his course clear, he has the courage to move. This is how *LOVE, PROXIMITY* and *COURAGE* ignite true change.

The Path of Pain

Sometimes, when we lose our way emotionally, it's helpful to have a map. The Path of Love describes the natural journey we are meant to take. The Path of Pain describes the journey we take when we stray from love, and the path we must take to return home.

THE PATH OF PAIN

For some reason, we come into this world with an expectation of being loved perfectly and unconditionally. We look up to our parents as gods, expecting them to know everything, to protect us from harm, to help us, and love us. And when they don't, the pain of that disappointment can create wounds deep enough to impact the rest of our lives.

Think about it. We don't come in expecting the world to be really bad and are then pleasantly surprised when it's not as bad as we thought. No, we come in expecting love, connection and wholeness. The truth is, love is all around us. It's just not always expressed.

Basing our expectations on unconditional love can set us up for a fall. This faulty thinking infiltrates our jobs, our friendships, and even our lives. *She expects that someone will be there for her and they're not. He expects that he will be treated fairly and he's not.* We enter relationships with unrealistic expectations. We expect the other person to be flawless; capable of providing unconditional love that even we, ourselves, cannot. The courtship goes well, everyone on best behavior and all. But when reality sets in and the other person stumbles, we are *disappointed*.

Each one of us comes into this lifetime with the concept of unconditional love embedded in our psyche. We could call it our blueprint for an ideal life – a picture of wholeness, love and peace. Perhaps that is what makes us strive for it the rest of our lives. In order to create such a world, we must realize that it is not something we will inherit. It is something we must bring.

At the core of pain is disappointment and behind the disappointment is expectations. By understanding the expectation we can address the disappointment and begin the healing. Often, however, before we catch the expectation, we've sauntered off down a path that begins with pain and ends with shame. Understanding the order as it unfolds, helps us understand the path we walk to return to love.

The Path of Pain

Love

Disappointment

Sadness

Fear

Anger

Shame

Love

We begin in a loving place, feeling connected to all things.

Disappointment

Something happens. Our expectations fail to be met at which point we feel pain. This causes us to move off center, away from love.

Sadness

Sadness is the first warning that we've drifted from love. As we veer off center, we lose focus. We begin to get double vision, to see ourselves as separate and disconnected. This creates a feeling of sadness, also known as grief or pain. Address the sadness and we return to love.

Fear

If we fail to address the sadness, the next warning we get is fear. Naturally, we feel afraid, seeing ourselves as separate and disconnected. We adopt the illusion that we are abandoned and left to fend for ourselves. In separation, we no longer have the benefit of being able to see the whole. We see only one side at a time, making us vulnerable to what we cannot see. If we address the fear and revisit the pain, we return to love or center.

Anger

Failing to return to love, the pain and fear increase and we must find some way to relieve the pressure of this disconnected and now dangerous world. The next feeling that arises is anger. With anger, we push the feelings outside of us and onto someone else. In other words, we blame. *It's their fault.* We feel a bit better, but with the blame, we inadvertently give away our power to change as well. If we address the anger, the fear dissipates, the pain resolves, and we return to love.

Shame

If we fail to return, we move to our last coping measure. That is shame. We must either shame the other person, alienating ourselves beyond repair, or we are shamed. Shame carries with it such an undesirable feeling that we take all memory of the experience and seal it away behind closed doors, never to be opened again - or so we hope. The problem with shame is that some part of it always leaks out. *He puts his shameful money problems behind him and yet every time he uses his credit card he feels anxiety over whether or not it will be accepted. She gets her shameful sexual behavior under control, but she always thinks nice people are judging her.*

At each step of the way, we have the opportunity to grow and resolve our thoughts and feelings. Fail to do so and they return more charged than the last time. Following the Path of Love, we grow and gain in awareness, strength and wisdom. Staying with love is the key to moving beyond our limitations and flying.

THE PATH OF LOVE

From a place of love, all things are possible. Life is abundant, creative, and meaningful. We are always supported, if we allow it. These are the experiences we must begin to reinforce to create more true change in our lives.

The Path of Love

Love

Experience

Acceptance

Growth

Change

Love

We begin in a loving place, feeling connected to all things.

Experience

We have an experience.

Acceptance

We accept it for what it is.

Growth

We learn from our experience and we grow.

Change

A new experience presents itself.

Shame

REALM: *The Soul*
CAUSE: *Intolerable pressure*
SELF-DEFEATING BELIEF:
I've done something terribly wrong.
COPING MECHANISM: *Denial*
TIME: *"It never existed"*
REAL MESSAGE: *It's time to become whole.*
QUESTION: *What part of yourself wants to re-connect?*

Sadness

REALM: *The Heart*
CAUSE: *Disappointment from false expectations*
SELF-DEFEATING BELIEF:
Abandonment. I'm on my own.
COPING MECHANISM: *The Freeze Frame*
TIME: *The Past*
REAL MESSAGE: *Get out of the past.*
QUESTION: *What are you holding onto?*

Love

Anger

REALM: *The Body*
CAUSE: *Paralyzed by fear*
SELF-DEFEATING BELIEF:
I'm powerless to change.
COPING MECHANISM: *Projection*
TIME: *Fluctuating between past and future*
REAL MESSAGE: *Something wants to change.*
QUESTION: *What wants to change?*

Fear

REALM: *The Mind*
CAUSE: *Belief in Separation*
SELF-DEFEATING BELIEF:
I'm not safe.
COPING MECHANISM: *Illusions and Lies*
TIME: *The Future*
REAL MESSAGE: *Get back to the truth*
QUESTION: *What lies are you believing?*

The Compass of Love

A Tool for Change

When we've wandered down the Path of Pain, it can often feel as if we've lost our way. To navigate our way back, we need the Compass of Love. No matter which juncture we're at – *sadness, fear, anger or shame* – there is a road that takes us back to love.

The Compass of Love is a process tool for change. Once a situation in our lives heats up, thoughts and feelings arise. We may not always know what to make of them, where they come from, or what to do with them. The Compass is there to help make sense of them. Each feeling will guide us back to love if we know how to interpret it. In the following pages we will look at what triggers the feelings, the coping mechanisms we've developed to deal with them, and their true messages. The Compass of Love is an ideal tool to sort out your feelings relative to a person or situation.

Once you've worked the issue, the way is clear to let love guide you. Here are a few questions to ask when you're ready to find out where Life will take you next:

Where's the joy?

What would make me happy right now?

What am I longing for?

What is calling to me from the world?

How near or far do I need to be from this person or situation to feel love in my heart?

SADNESS

As with the Path of Pain, the first step away from Love is sadness. An expectation we have is unmet. We're disappointed, leaving us feeling alone and abandoned.

The coping mechanism we have for sadness is the *freeze frame*. We freeze the moment with the intention of returning when we're better equipped to deal with the pain. Every time we find ourselves in a similar situation, we have the opportunity to handle it differently. Ideally, the older we get, the more skills we acquire and the more able we are of doing things differently.

When I was a small child I had an unfortunate experience with a man in my friend's neighborhood. I wanted someone to rescue me. Afterward, I wanted someone to ask me if I was okay. But that never happened since no one knew about it.

I blanked this experience out until years later, but its influence did not go away. The next thirty years of my life were shaped by the unmet need to be rescued. As a teenager I spent many hours alone in my room, waiting for someone to look for me. In my 20's, I married a man who was addicted to drugs, subconsciously hoping someone would come and pull me away. In fact, my parents did, but that's a funny thing about the *freeze frame*. It's frozen in time. Even if the situation is closely re-enacted, it doesn't release it. Somewhere inside, we're holding onto the need for the exact person to fix the exact situation which, of course, can never happen. The only way out, is to provide for ourselves what we needed from someone else. When we do, we're healed.

After a life of many desperate experiences, I remember a moment when I realized I could take care of myself. Instead of feeling happy, the thought occurred to me that if I did that, I would be alone. I wouldn't need anyone else to rescue me. In other words, needing to be rescued was a way of maintaining a connection. I decided then and there that I wanted whatever connections I had, to be ones of joy and happiness instead of need and desperation.

When we feel sadness or grief, we are put on notice that we're holding onto something from the past. It's time to let go. To work with grief, we've got to stop running and allow the past to catch up with us. The image I get is someone running through a forest, their clothes snagging on branches and limbs. They keep running, but threads of the fabric are stuck behind. The more they run, the more the fabric tears, and the more difficult it is to go.

When trying to move through sadness, good questions to ask are: Who or what do I feel separated from? Who's love am I waiting for? What am I holding onto?

Re-interpreting SADNESS

Our answer to sadness is the freeze-frame.

We pause painful moments, hoping some day we can make them right.

The real message of sadness is: Get out of the past.

REALM: The Heart

CAUSE: Disappointment from false expectations

SELF-DEFEATING BELIEF: Abandonment. I'm on my own.

COPING MECHANISM: The Freeze Frame

TIME: The Past

TRUE MESSAGE: Get out of the past.

POWERFUL QUESTIONS:

    Who or what do I feel disconnected from?

    Who's love am I waiting for?

    What am I holding onto from the past?

    What am I disappointed about?

    What expectation has not been met?

    Was that expectation realistic?

    What would a more realistic expectation be?

FEAR

What is required with sadness is to go through it. What we often do, however, is move away from it. Then we lie to ourselves so we can endure it. *It's not that bad. Maybe he'll come back. She didn't really mean it. It'll be better tomorrow. I didn't really want that anyway.* All the while, a feeling of anguish builds. We know we're on shaky ground.

In order to believe these lies, the message we really have to accept is that life does not work. There is not enough love, abundance, joy, nurturing, or support. Life is lack. From here, life becomes a scary place with an underlying belief that we are not safe. Homelessness and starvation are just around the corner. Greed lives here. We must store up so we have enough.

Using the Compass of Love, we can turn fear around. The true message of fear is: Get back to the truth. Some powerful questions are: What lies am I believing about how life works? What lies am I believing about myself or someone else right now? What is the truth about this situation?

Re-interpreting FEAR

We lie to ourselves so we can endure the pain.

In order to believe these lies, we accept the message that Life is lack.

From there, life becomes a scary place.

The real message of fear is: Get back to the truth.

REALM: The Mind

CAUSE: Belief in Separation

SELF-DEFEATING BELIEF: I'm not safe.

COPING MECHANISM: Illusions or Lies

TIME: The Future

TRUE MESSAGE: Get back to the truth.

POWERFUL QUESTIONS:

What lies am I believing about how Life works?

What lies am I believing about myself or someone else right now?

What is the truth about this situation?

Who or what do I feel unsafe with?

Where do I feel paralyzed with fear?

ANGER

Instead of creating movement, we become paralyzed by fear. Meanwhile, the pressure for healing continues to build. Unable to make a change ourselves, we start looking for what else might give way. Thus, we come to projection. When the pain becomes too great, the coping mechanism is to get it outside of ourselves and project it onto someone else. Instead of thinking, *I've got to do something,* we think, *Why don't they do something!* This often results in a stalemate. You won't change. They won't change. Nobody changes…and the pressure keeps building. Herein lies a recipe for war.

The Compass of Love shows us a way through. When we feel angry, the true interpretation is: Something wants to change. The helpful questions are: What wants to change? Who or what have I given my power to? What part of this situation am I responsible for?

Re-interpreting ANGER

We project the need for change onto someone or something else

when we're too stuck to make it ourselves.

By doing so, we inadvertently give our power away.

The real message of anger is: Something wants to change.

REALM: The Body

CAUSE: Paralyzed by fear

SELF-DEFEATING BELIEF: I'm powerless to change.

COPING MECHANISM: Projection

TIME: Fluctuating between past and future

TRUE MESSAGE: Something wants to change.

POWERFUL QUESTIONS:

    What wants to change?

    Who or what have I given my power to?

    What part of this situation am I responsible for?

    What do I risk by making this change?

    How do I get to stay "small" by keeping things the same?

SHAME

At this point, someone usually does something they'll regret. They lash out, break off ties, quit or something worse. They have drifted so far from love that it is a distant memory. They forget about why they loved the other person or why they loved their situation. They forget that we are all in this together.

We can point the finger at the other person, but, in the end, even when we win, we lose. Buried deep within is a feeling that we've done something terribly wrong. We keep up a good face, but in a parallel world, we sense that a frightening part of ourselves is just waiting to surface.

In order to return to wholeness, we must acknowledge our shame. This can be difficult. Shame is so ashamed of itself that it hides. In order to find it, we must be fierce warriors, unafraid of the "horrors" we might find or the pain we may suffer. In my experience, the thought of it is always much worse than the reality.

Shame tells us it's time to unlock the door and face our demons. Surprisingly, what we find underneath the façade of a really "horrible person", is someone we love – us. Freedom from shame requires two things: acknowledgement and forgiveness. *I made a poor choice and I forgive myself.*

The true message of shame is that there is a banished part of ourselves wanting to come home. Helpful questions include: What part of myself wants to re-connect? What positive part of myself am I afraid to employ? What am I afraid I will do, say or be?

Re-interpreting SHAME

In shame, love is a distant memory.

Buried deep within is a feeling that we've done something terribly wrong.

Shame tells us it's time to unlock the door and face our demons.

The real message of shame is: Time to reclaim a lost part of yourself.

REALM: Soul

CAUSE: Intolerable pressure

SELF-DEFEATING BELIEF: I've done something terribly wrong.

COPING MECHANISM: Denial

TIME: "It never existed"

TRUE MESSAGE: Time to reclaim a lost part of yourself.

POWERFUL QUESTIONS:

What part of myself wants to be re-connected?

What part of myself am I afraid to re-activate?

What am I afraid I will do, say or be?

What truth have I been denying about myself or someone else?

USING THE COMPASS OF LOVE

The formula for creating transformative change is:

Come from a place of love,

Wait for clarity, and,

Have the courage to act when the way is clear.

The Compass of Love is a great tool if you get stuck along the way. Here's how to use it.

Start by writing down the name of the person or situation you want to explore.

1. Now, sense which emotion you feel the most –sadness, fear, anger, or shame.

2. Look up that feeling on the Compass.

3. Read the true message and consider how this applies to your situation.

4. Ask yourself the powerful questions and write down your answers.

5. Check the Compass for the coping mechanism and see how you might be using it to cover up rather than clarify.

Once you've gained some insight into the first feeling, sense which feeling is most prevalent next. Go through the five steps above. Continue this process, working each of the four directions.

By the end of this process, you will have brought all of your thoughts and feelings on the subject out of the shadow and into the light. With a clear perspective, you will have the energy for change. Now it's time to turn to Love and find out where it's guiding you. Explore these questions:

Where's the joy?

What would make me happy right now?

What am I longing for?

What is calling to me from the world?

How near or far do I need to be from this person or situation to feel love in my heart?

Vision

Together we Rise

Almost every culture has a story of a golden age, or paradise, when the beings who inhabited the earth lived in an idyllic and magical state. These stories, found in the ancient records of many indigenous cultures, tell of a time of harmony not only with each other but with all life – the cosmos, the animals, the plants, and the earth itself. In these legends, we were luminous, creator beings who, in many cases, could even fly.

Coupled with the stories of paradise are legends of a fall, the descent into a state of collective amnesia in which we forgot our true identity. We became separate from our true selves seeing the world in polarity: either/or, right or wrong, good or bad, up or down. It's not important for us to agree on whether these stories are fact or fiction. We need only look around to see that we are out of alignment with our world. How else could we hurt one another and destroy the very home upon which we live?

As we rapidly run through natural resources destroying entire ecosystems, the pressure is building to find a more sustainable relationship with our world. We are beginning to understand what it means to be a global community, but the more connected we are, the more complex the interrelatedness becomes. We help some and hurt others, fix one thing only to negatively impact something else. Trying to sort out our affairs at this level is challenging at best.

In the legends of a golden age and a fall, there is one last part to the story - the prophesy of a return to paradise. They refer to a world reunited from the separation we have known, a world created together in synch with one another and in synch with Life itself. Rumi, a Sufi poet, spoke of it as a field beyond right and wrong. He said, "I'll meet you there."

A SUSTAINABLE FUTURE

This may seem like a tall order. In fact, it is not that complicated. The answer has nothing to do with trying to change the world, but of creating a new reality. In the first, the changes take place in the physical. In the second, the transformation occurs within ourselves and alters how we experience the world. In this new reality, we choose love, truth, and life.

> ### *The answer has nothing to do with trying to change the world, but of creating a new reality.*

There's never been a truer statement than "Love makes the world go 'round." When we come from a place of love, we honor the Life that's moving through us. We follow the urges and they guide and move us. Things change for ourselves and everyone around us.

When we speak our truth, the world around us has the opportunity to listen. When we stand up for ourselves, those around us are given the opportunity to respond. Not speaking our truth, the world goes on living a lie. Opting out on the chance to speak up and take our space in the world, the world is less than what it might be. Failing to follow through on Life's guidance, we wander in the wilderness, hopelessly lost. Inspired by Life, we live. We make sense out of the chaos. The pieces fall into place. The world changes, not by our whim or weakness, but by a coordinated design.

Albert Einstein once suggested that problems cannot be solved at the same level of consciousness that created them. Choices made in separation result in more separation. From that perspective we see only more of the same.

To change paradigms, we must drop ballast and rise up, suspending what we know long enough to perceive a new path. This doesn't mean that we all see things the same way. In fact, it means that all of the facets are revealed, the beautiful differentiation of love made manifest in our unique ways, all together.

A RENEWABLE RESOURCE CALLED LOVE

As we cast out fear and bitterness, choosing to align instead with Love, we come into alignment with Life. This alignment has the power to transform the world. We no longer make arbitrary choices based on unconscious, wounded needs but powerful choices orchestrated by Life itself. These choices act in coordination with all life. Our inter-connectedness becomes a reality. We know that what benefits one, blesses us all. What harms one, dooms us all. But better than that is the fact that we needn't have all of the answers. We needn't be omnipotent. We merely need to be aligned with something real like love and the rest of the world begins to shake out around us.

As we cast out fear and bitterness, choosing to align instead with Love, we come into alignment with Life. This alignment has the power to transform the world.

Life works. We can count on this. When we cease resisting and come into the flow, our lives work, too. It's as simple as that. We have the power to turn the tide of any situation merely by changing the way we experience it. This process of *LOVE, PROXIMITY* and *COURAGE* is a means of repairing the old circuitry and re-wiring back to Life. It helps us fully participate in the creative process. To do this, we re-sensitize to feelings and use them to navigate our way back to love, or center. We liberate the mind from illusions held in place by the ego. And we have the courage to act when the path is laid before us.

The more adept we become at this process, the more consistent we become. Keeping the flame alive, we continuously burn away that which is no longer useful and come into step with Life. We remember to check our emotions and re-align with Love. We know that we can always adjust proximity to gain the proper perspective. And we have the tools to find the courage for change when the time arrives.

Conscious living becomes a way of life. This is another way of saying that we begin living in the present moment. And it is only in the moment that anyone can truly know what needs to happen next. We can think and plan and strategize, but no one can know exactly what factors will present themselves in that moment - until you're there. Then and only then will our intuition guide us.

TOGETHER WE RISE

It isn't necessary for others to cooperate in order for one's reality to change. That happens internally, independent of anyone else. But imagine for a moment what it would be like to have two or more people in the moment breathing the same breath…flowing in the same river… callings and longings intersecting…holding steady…until birth is given to something more profound than what was ever possible alone.

This is how the ills of the world will be restored. Not with minds driven by our collective unconscious, but by allowing new options to emerge from our collective hearts and minds aligned.

Nobel laureate and Former Vice President Al Gore describes this collective experience in an article he wrote for *Vanity Fair* magazine entitled *The Moment of Truth*. Relative to global warming, he says:

This crisis is bringing us an opportunity to experience what few generations in history ever have the privilege of knowing: a generational mission; the exhilaration of a compelling moral purpose; a shared and unifying cause; the thrill of being forced by circumstances to put aside the pettiness and conflict that so often stifle the restless human need for transcendence; the opportunity to rise.

When we do rise, it will fill our spirits and bind us together. Those who are now suffocating in cynicism and despair will be able to breathe freely. Those who are now suffering from a loss of meaning in their lives will find hope.

When we rise, we will experience an epiphany as we discover that this crisis is not really about politics at all. It is a moral and spiritual challenge.

When we rise, we are treated to a higher perspective. From this place, we can more clearly see what is real and what is an illusion. We have been wandering in the wilderness of the unconscious, unaware that we have lost our way. We find ourselves banished to the world of opposites, the land of either/or in which something is always missing all the while overlooking the fact that endless possibilities exist.

We can try to resist the very forces of the Universe or we can let go into the dance. Willing to stand in the fire, we come into synch with one another. Doors open. Life clicks. Magic happens. Ascending to higher ground, the world begins to shift from what we have to what we only imagined it could be. The chains of pain and suffering are broken and we begin to know life as it was meant to be – ignited and free!

RESOURCES

A Little Book on the Human Shadow, by Robert Bly. New York: HarperOne, 1988

The Art of Pilgrimage, by Phil Cousineau. Berkeley, California: Conari Press, 2000

Getting the Love You Want, by Harville Hendrix. New York: Holt Paperbacks, 2007

King, Warrior, Magician, Lover, by Robert Moore and Douglas Gillette. San Francisco, California: HarperOne, 1991

Loving What Is, by Byron Katie. New York: Three Rivers Press, 2003

Memories and Visions of Paradise, by Richard Heinberg. JP Tarcher, 1990

Nonviolent Communication: A Language of Life, by Marshall Rosenberg. Encinitas, California: PuddleDancer Press, 2003. www.cnvc.org

Owning Your Own Shadow, by Robert A. Johnson. San Francisco: HarperOne, 1993

The Places That Scare You, by Pema Chödrön. Boston: Shambhala Publications, Inc., 2007

Spiritual Enlightenment, the Damnedest Thing, by Jed McKenna. Wisefool Press, 2002

Time and the Soul, by Jacob Needleman. San Francisco: Berrett-Koehler Publishers, 2003

The Universe is a Green Dragon, by Brian Swimme. Santa Fe, NM: Bear & Company, 1984

Woman of the Ages: Regaining Our Ancient Memory, by Dr. Frances M. Pastoria. Authorhouse, 2006

Shadow Work®, is a way to bring your true self out of shadow and into the light. It includes a set of facilitated processes that allow individuals to explore and change almost any behavior pattern.

SunDo is a form of Taoist Korean yoga handed down over the last 9800 years. It has only been in the last 35 years that this practice was re-introduced into mainstream culture. www.sundo.org

ANNA FRANCESCA CELESTINO couples thirty years of spiritual training with numerous years in the entertainment industry to bring timeless information in a light and accessible way. Her healing and life coaching practice has assisted thousands to move through difficult blocks. She has been facilitating personal development since 1993.

Anna is available for private sessions, life coaching, talks, and workshops. She can be reached at: anna@ignitingchange.com

For free worksheets and additional resources
to ignite change in your life, visit
www.IgnitingChange.com

2788926

Made in the USA